Twayne's United States Authors Series

Sylvia E. Bowman, *Editor*

INDIANA UNIVERSITY

Laurence Stallings

TUSAS 250

Laurence Stallings

LAURENCE STALLINGS

By JOAN T. BRITTAIN

Bellarmine College

TWAYNE PUBLISHERS

A DIVISION OF G. K. HALL & CO., BOSTON

Library of Congress Cataloging in Publication Data

Brittain, Joan T   1928-
  Laurence Stallings.

  (Twayne's United States authors series ; TUSAS 250)
  Bibliography: p. 123-26.
  Includes index.
  1. Stallings, Laurence, 1894 - 1968.
PS3537.T164Z59   813'.5'2 [B]   74-23831
ISBN 0-8057-0686-0

To Harvey and Hal

Contents

About the Author

A native of Manchester, Georgia, Joan T. Brittain attended LaGrange College, LaGrange, Georgia, in 1945-47, married, reared four children, and returned to college at the age of 35. In 1965, she received her Bachelor of Arts Degree with honors in English from Kentucky Southern College, Louisville, and was awarded a teaching fellowship at the University of Louisville. There she completed the Master of Arts in 1966 and the Ph.D. in December, 1970. In 1967 she was elected to Phi Kappa Phi National Honor Society.

While still a graduate student, Dr. Brittain published numerous articles for such literary periodicals as *Renascence, Explicator,* and *Bulletin of Bibliography.* She joined the faculty of Bellarmine College in 1967 but continued her graduate studies while also co-authoring *The Eternal Crossroads; The Art of Flannery O'Connor* (University Press of Kentucky, 1971).

Awarded the "Younger Humanist Fellowship" for 1972 - 73 by the National Endowment for the Humanities, Dr. Brittain was also elected that year to "Outstanding Educators of America."

As Associate Professor of English at Bellarmine College, Louisville, she teaches the novel, advanced composition, modern drama, and American literature. Director of the "Phoenix Program" for high-risk students, she spent four summers working with the Upward Bound program, sponsored by the Office of Economic Opportunity. There are now students in colleges in all parts of the United States who had their first college course in Dr. Brittain's Upward Bound classes.

Preface

It is generally acknowledged that World War I had a greater impact on American writers than any single event of the century and that during the 1920's American writers produced a volume of literary works based on that war and its aftermath. Some few, like Willa Cather in *One of Ours* (1922), interpreted the experience as a great heroic adventure; but, for others, it was a traumatic experience and was treated as such by many authors who responded with profound disillusionment or disappointment. John Dos Passos in *Three Soldiers* (1921), E. E. Cummings in *The Enormous Room* (1922), Thomas Boyd in *Through the Wheat* (1923), Laurence Stallings in *Plumes* and (with Maxwell Anderson) *What Price Glory?* (1924), William Faulkner in *Soldiers' Pay* (1926), and Ernest Hemingway in *The Sun Also Rises* (1926) and in *A Farewell to Arms* (1929) had surprisingly similar reactions.

With the exception of Laurence Stallings and, perhaps, Thomas Boyd, these authors and their works are well known to students of American literature. Yet, of these American writer-veterans (and Willa Cather was "over there"), Laurence Stallings was one of the most famous during the 1920's. Uniquely, his interest in *the War* (at least to his generation) continued throughout his publishing career, 1924-1963. Perhaps the experience of war affected him more deeply because he suffered a greater personal involvement than that of other writers, for Stallings was seriously wounded in combat and eventually lost both legs as a result. Steeped in the Southern Romantic lore of his past, he had, like many others, entered the war as a naive youth. He was ill-equipped for the bloody confrontation, and that fact, too, made the hell of it all the more savage for him. The experience left him traumatized psychically and affected his major literary output to the extent that he continually dealt with war. Indeed, Stallings was the only American author who based all his major work on World War I. He was, however, a veteran of both world wars and that alone distinguishes him from other writers concerned with war.

My primary purpose in this study is to introduce Laurence Stallings to students of American literature through a consideration of his life and work; and, in doing so, center specifically on Stallings' conflicting attitudes toward war as he examined such conflict not only in the novel and the drama but also in short stories, film scenarios, essays, newspaper articles, and interpretive histories. This wide range of work indicates some of the problems inherent in this study. For example, his stories, published in the 1920's and 1930's, have never been collected. His newspaper articles, also from the 1920's and 1930's, total more than eight hundred and are available on microfilm only. *Plumes* has long been difficult to find because Stallings never allowed it to be reprinted after 1925, and we wonder if a writer ever tried more deliberately to kill a book of such obvious merit. Magazine articles that Stallings wrote as a war correspondent are scattered and unindexed. Few film scenarios are available. After 1932 he published no new fiction; but his story "Vale of Tears" (1931), of which he was extremely proud, was anthologized by Ernest Hemingway in *Men at War* (1942) and was reissued as late as 1955. *The First World War: A Pictorial History* (1933,1962) and the interpretive chronicle, *The Doughboys* (1963), are still available.

Because of the general inaccessibility of much of Stallings' work, extended explication seems a necessary part of my approach. Most importantly, a detailed explication of *Plumes* is required to show Stallings' artistic ability to communicate effectively — and poetically — with structural unity. The major works seem to form one whole, the germs of which can be traced back to and through this novel as well as interrelated with the life of the man. Then too, the complexity of Stallings' shifting attitudes of disillusionment and reconciliation are best understood through contextual analysis. Direct relationships can be established between such personal attitudes and the basic elements of his craft — imagery, symbolism, characterization, setting, tone, and style. Pertinent biographical facts shed light on the literary works; for, unlike some writers who have difficulty discovering their own literary mode, Stallings began successfully in 1924 and continued to write autobiographically in seven different literary forms. Such an accomplishment reflects the man's versatility. Yet no genre, apparently, ever claimed him.

Preface

As I have indicated, no major work on Stallings exists. There are, of course, reviews of all his publications; occasional appraisals by such perceptive critics as Joseph Wood Krutch, Malcolm Cowley, and Kenneth Burke exist; but no balanced picture of the man-artist he really was has been presented. In the 1920's and 1930's great claims were made for Stallings; for example, one critic, who compared him to Carl Sandburg, wrote: "Laurence Stallings and Carl Sandburg are as sure to live in the literary history of this country as any two men now writing."[1] And Archibald MacLeish called *Plumes* "one of the few novels of our time which can be said to have a real expectancy of life."[2] But Stallings is rarely mentioned today in anthologies of American literature. He does, however, deserve consideration for his contribution as a writer-veteran of both world wars who became historian and patriot.

JOAN T. BRITTAIN

Bellarmine College

Acknowledgments

Grateful acknowledgment is made to the following for permission to quote copyrighted material in this book:

American Heritage Publishing Company for permission to quote from Laurence Stallings, "The War to End War" (1959).

Harcourt Brace Jovanovich, Inc. for permission to quote from Laurence Stallings, *Plumes* (1924, 1952); Maxwell Anderson and Laurence Stallings, *Three American Plays* (1926, 1954).

Harper and Row, Publishers, Inc. for permission to quote from Laurence Stallings, *The Doughboys* (1963).

King Vidor for permission to quote from King Vidor, *A Tree Is a Tree* (1952).

Special thanks go to Mrs. Laurence Stallings for her cooperation and permission to use the published works for this study; to Mrs. Helen Poteat Marshall for verifying biographical data and for sharing the library at "Forest Home"; to Mr. Arthur Krock for providing a considerable amount of correspondence; to Mr. and Mrs. Roland Neel for their tour of Macon, Georgia, and their help in locating biographical data; to Mr. George Kilcourse for collecting titles of newspaper articles on microfilm at the New York Public Library; to Mrs. Ilona Franck, Bellarmine College librarian, for purchasing primary sources and collecting material through interlibrary loan; and to Mrs. Dorothea Marks and Mrs. Virginia Callan for typing the manuscript.

To the many who provided or verified biographical information I wish to express thanks. Some of these include: Mrs. Preston Witherspoon, Mrs. William F. Hobby, Jr., Mr. George B. Stallings, Dr. Frank Vandiver, Mr. King Vidor, Mr. Walter Lippmann, Mrs. Beatrice Pope, Mrs. Charlotte Bowers, Miss Minnie Kallam, Mr. H. N. Swanson, Professor H. Edward Richardson, Mr. Lowell Thomas,

Acknowledgments

Mr. Archibald MacLeish, Mr. Max Wyeth, Mr. Robert Lovett, and Senator Marlow Cook.

Additional information or material was furnished by the Library of Congress, the National Archives, the Academy of Motion Picture Arts and Sciences, Metro-Goldwyn-Mayer, Warner Brothers-Seven Arts, Twentieth Century Fox Film Corporation, the Atlanta Board of Education and the Atlanta *Journal*, the Bibb County Board of Education and the *Macon Telegraph and News*, Macon, Georgia. Thank you for your help.

Most of all I am grateful to Dr. Robert A. Preston, Academic Vice President and Dean of Bellarmine College, for his cooperation and encouragement and for allowing me the time to complete this work.

Chronology

1894 Laurence Tucker Stallings born in Macon, Georgia, November 25.

1911 Graduated from Gresham High School, Macon, Georgia; the Stallings family moved to Atlanta, Georgia.

1912- Attended Wake Forest College at Wake Forest, North
1915 Carolina.

1915 Joined the staff of the Atlanta *Journal* as a reporter.

1916 Received Bachelor of Arts degree from Wake Forest.

1917 Appointed Second Lieutenant in the United States Marine Corps; trained at Parris Island, South Carolina.

1918 Wounded on June 26 at Belleau Wood, France.

1919 Returned to United States in February. Married to Helen Poteat on March 6.

1920 Placed on list of retired officers, June 28. He and wife settled in Washington, D.C. Stallings joined staff of the Washington *Times*.

1922 Right leg amputated in February at Walter Reed Hospital. Began work on *Plumes*. After release from hospital, traveled in Europe; on return, settled in New York City. Joined staff of New York *World*.

1924 *What Price Glory?* produced. Published *Plumes* and "The Big Parade."

1925 *First Flight* and *The Buccaneer* produced. Stallings revisited site of World War I injury.

1926 Left the New York *World;* settled in North Carolina.

1928 First child, Sylvia, born. Published "Esprit de corps," "Turn Out the Guard"; collaborated with Oscar Hammerstein, II, on musical *Rainbow*.

1930 Dramatized for the stage Ernest Hemingway's *A Farewell to Arms*.

1931   Became literary editor for New York *Sun.* Published "Vale of Tears."

1932   Second child, Diana, born. Published "Gentleman in Blue," "Return to the Woods," and *The First World War: A Pictorial History.*

1934   Became editor of Fox Movietonews.

1935   Became literary editor of *American Mercury.* Headed news and newsreel team in Ethiopia.

1936   Became associate editor of *American Mercury.* Divorced by Helen Poteat on December 1.

1937   Married Louise St. Leger Vance on March 19. Couple settled in Santa Barbara, California.

1939   First son, Laurence, Jr., born March 6.

1941   Fourth and last child, Sally, born September 5.

1942   Recalled to active military duty on April 2. "Vale of Tears" anthologized by Ernest Hemingway in *Men at War.*

1943   Retired with rank of lieutenant-colonel on June 27. Family settled in Whittier, California.

1944   *The Streets Are Guarded* produced.

1959   Published "The War to End War."

1962   *The First World War: A Pictorial History* reissued.

1963   Published *The Doughboys.* Second leg amputated.

1964   Honored for service to his country, June 24.

1968   Died of heart attack on February 29.

CHAPTER 1

"A Genius"

A RTHUR Krock, noted journalist, once said of Laurence
Stallings: "He was a genius, and we never understand a
genius."[1] Indeed, it is difficult to understand a man whose literary
works expose war's horror and absurdity but whose personal fascination for war might even be likened to Ahab's pursuit of the white
whale. Whether or not Stallings ever understood his own attraction
to numerous encounters with death one cannot say, but Stallings
never said, "I love war." Conversely, he reflected his hatred of it as
he rebelled against its destruction and the fact that mankind never
learns anything from history.

I *Background in Georgia*

Influencing at least one historian, Frank E. Vandiver, who also
thought Stallings a "man of remarkable capacity and genius,"[2]
Stallings was proudest of his own historical chronicle, *The
Doughboys.* But his lifelong concern with history began — to borrow
a phrase from his novel *Plumes* — with "a diet of shining swords" in
Macon, Georgia. There he was born on November 25, 1894, to
Aurora Brooks and Larkin Tucker Stallings, a collecting teller for the
First National Bank. Laurence was the youngest of three children:
his brother, George Brooks, is now dead; his sister, Ruth (Mrs.
Preston Witherspoon) lives in New York. Stallings' maternal grand-
parents were Dr. and Mrs. George Washington Brooks of Dothan,
Alabama. His paternal grandparents were the Reverend and Mrs.
Jesse Stallings, of Stallings, South Carolina. The Reverend Stallings
was a Baptist minister, "from a long line of Baptist ministers";[3] and
Dr. Brooks was a surgeon. Neither of the grandfathers fought in the
Civil War, but the Reverend Jesse Stallings lost two brothers in the
war. Ironically, other surgeons and other Baptist ministers played
important roles in Stallings' life; but his mother impressed him most.

A tall, striking woman who loved music and books, she dominated the household.

Stallings' father was a shy, quiet man who, by 1903, was promoted to general bookkeeper at the bank. With the promotion came a move from Johnson Avenue near Mercer University to 221 Forsyth Street, now renumbered 1337, where the family lived until they left Macon. On Forsyth Street Stallings enjoyed the youthful camaraderie of neighbors Champney Holmes and Roland Neel, now a prominent citizen and civic leader of Macon.[4] Several blocks from the boyhood home stands a tall, imposing statue of a Confederate soldier; we can easily imagine young Laurence standing before it and admiring the uniform and the hat cocked on the side of the head. Throughout his life, he loved uniforms and hats; and he eventually wrote a story, "Gentleman in Blue," about a boy's fascination with these things — cockade hats, in particular.

But for three young "soldiers" engaging in rock fights in an area nicknamed the "battleground" — two blocks from home — there were no such accoutrements. Mainly armed with vivid imaginations, the youths engaged in such activities as making arrows out of metal umbrella spokes to shoot at passing buggies. They also enjoyed building bonfires at nearby Magnolia Park where they always attended Confederate Memorial Day and Fourth of July parades — impressive sights that are described in Stallings' fiction. But one of their favorite and more daring sports was running along railroad tracks as they raced the train across a trestle built over Monroe Street, one block from their homes. Physical pursuits were, however, accompanied by a desire for knowledge, and Stallings as a very young boy was especially curious about words. According to his sister, Ruth, he "never let a printed word escape his attention; he even read labels on medicine bottles. He read everything he could get."

Especially interested in Civil War history, particularly General Sherman's march through Georgia, young Stallings enjoyed stories of the historic past which were as prevalent in Macon as the statues in honor of Civil War heroes. Though spared Civil War destruction, Macon was first known as Fort Hawkins, a replica of which still stands at the corner of Maynard Avenue and Emery Highway. Built in 1806 by a government Indian agent, Benjamin Hawkins, Fort Hawkins and its history were well known. From this base in 1817, Andrew Jackson led his troops against the Creek Indians. As a boy, Stallings and his two friends hunted Indian arrowheads and played "war" there while Stallings mentally recorded material which he used later in his writing.

II *At Wake Forest*

A good student, Stallings was graduated from Gresham High School in 1911, and shortly afterward his family moved to Atlanta, Georgia, where his father became treasurer of a wholesale drug company. Young Laurence worked for less than a year as a clerk at the Royal Insurance Company before he left in 1912 to attend Wake Forest College, a small Baptist liberal arts college in Wake Forest, North Carolina, where his education was financed by the Reverend John E. White, a Baptist minister and a close friend of Stallings' father. Stallings majored in classical studies and in biology; and his interest in both the humanities and sciences continued throughout his life. Stallings played football, another continuing interest and one described in *Plumes* as "a savage pleasure . . . a struggle for survival."[5] He also began writing in college; during his senior year he served as editor of the literary magazine, *The Old Gold and Black.*

While at Wake Forest, Stallings met his first wife, Helen Poteat, the daughter of his favorite biology professor and president of the college, Dr. William Louis Poteat. His son, Hubert, taught Stallings the classics. Almost a half century later, Stallings could enthusiastically recall those days at Wake Forest which were so important to him. He described his classes as the "rock" of his "erudition," and of his classmates he said: " . . . I don't recall a student who was not *playing the game* for keeps."[6] He regarded Dr. William Louis Poteat as a "marvelous dramatist and a great evangelist," but he was equally impressed with Dr. Poteat's successful efforts to defeat legislation prohibiting the teaching of evolution in North Carolina. (These efforts he labeled "Poteatism" in an article for the New York *World,* but in his novel *Plumes* "Poteatism" becomes "Bibbism.")

Stallings also recalled college escapades, such as getting caught drinking beer from a five-gallon keg that he and six others had hidden in a creek near the campus. His love of alcoholic beverages later earned him the nickname overseas of "Ice Water," but at Wake Forest he was known as "Giftie," and he was described in a Wake Forest publication, *The Howler* (1916), as "the widest read man in college." Never quite able to resist a practical joke or taking a gamble for a good time, Stallings, according to his first wife, was once expelled from the college for painting a nude statue that stood on campus. But he has spoken of his inability to fool anyone — academically at least — at Wake Forest. Describing Hubert Poteat as one who "struck terror in him early in the game," Stallings told of his punishment for using a "pony." Dr. Poteat sent him to the library to read the following scriptural quotation from the Second Book of Kings: "The horse is a vain thing for safety; nor shall he deliver any one by his strength." Stallings concluded this anecdote with, "I never used a pony again. And I believe . . . that I averaged out a 95 for the four Latin years."[7] Though Stallings received a bachelor of arts degree in 1916, he had actually completed his course work in 1915. He later included, only slightly altered, the setting, the people, and his experience at college in his novel *Plumes*.

III *Enlistment and Service*

In 1915, Stallings returned to Atlanta, where Major John Cohen, former war correspondent during the Spanish American War and later editor and president of the Atlanta *Journal*, gave Stallings his first reporting job. During this time he served with his father's old outfit of the National Guard; but on May 29, 1917, Stallings joined the Marine Corps Reserve at Atlanta and was assigned to active duty on July 25. He "was disenrolled on 9 October 1917, as a Private, to accept appointment as a Second Lieutenant in the regular Marine Corps," an appointment which began October 10.[8] He enlisted for five years in the Fifth Marines and left for Parris Island, South Carolina.

A handsome young man, Stallings stood over six feet tall in his uniform and was especially proud of being a Marine. He could hardly wait to get "over there," into action, and in 1918 he sailed to France with the Second Division, Forty-seventh Company, Third Battalion, of the Fifth Marines. He saw heavy action at Chateau-Thierry, leading that "first wave" of attack in Belleau Wood.[9] Stallings escaped injury until the last day of battle at Belleau, June 26. He spent the next eight months in a French hospital undergoing a series of operations to save his right leg. Roland Neel, recalling his friend's personal account of that wound, summarized the incident:

Stallings went after a machine gun nest that had to be wiped out. He gave each of his men two grenades, but he got closer than any of them. A bullet caught him in the right leg and ripped off his kneecap. He went down, but he threw the grenade anyway and wiped out the entire nest. When he came to, he was in the hospital, and he begged the doctor to save his leg. The doctor said he'd have to amputate, but Stallings told him he'd take full responsibility. He was determined to keep that leg, so the doctor inserted a bone and made him a stiff leg. For that wound he received the Croix de Guerre and a Silver Star.[10]

Stallings returned home a captain in February, 1919, and was transported to the Naval Hospital in Brooklyn. But he was out in time to get married on March 6. After he was placed on the list of retired officers on June 28, 1920, he and his wife, Helen, settled in Washington, D.C., so that the doctors at Walter Reed Hospital could "keep an eye on him."[11] Stallings spent part of the time in Washington doing odd reporting jobs for the Washington *Times.* Then, in 1922, after a bad fall on ice which tore the surgeon's repair work on his leg, Stallings returned to Walter Reed for the amputation of his right leg. (His second leg was not amputated until 1963.)

IV *In New York and Hollywood*

After his release from the hospital, Stallings and his wife left for Europe where Stallings worked on his novel *Plumes,* which he had begun in the hospital while recuperating in 1922. When they returned to this country, they settled in New York; and Stallings joined the staff of the New York *World* as a copy reader. In a short time, the editor, Herbert Bayard Swope, made Stallings drama critic; but the physical difficulty in being an itinerant reporter forced Stallings to seek another position. When Arthur Krock, then assistant to publisher Ralph Pulitzer, heard of Stallings' troubles, Krock persuaded Pulitzer to give Stallings the sedentary job of book reviewer on the "Op Ed Page" (opposite editorial page); and Stallings became "The First Reader." His column by that name appeared four times a week, but his name also appeared irregularly under four other columns. During his first year at the *World,* Stallings published more than four hundred articles. He worked with such writers as Heywood Broun, Franklin P. Adams, Deems Taylor, and Alexander Woollcott.

All of these writers, including Laurence Stallings, were "charter members of the Algonquin Round Table,"[12] as were George S. Kaufman, Robert Benchley, Harold Ross, Robert E. Sherwood, Dorothy Parker, Edna Ferber, Marc Connelly, and others. But Stallings was the only member who had been seriously hurt during the war and "was pretty much revered as a hero, although he did everything possible to discourage such reverence."[13] According to Margaret

Case Harriman, the group, composed mostly of young struggling writers, met at her father's hotel where they enjoyed stimulating conversation and games of all kinds, particularly word games. She describes the group as "crusaders" who hated shoddy work of any kind and who demanded accuracy of themselves and other writers: "When the members of the Vicious Circle were not crusading about something outside their particular fields, their own work amounted to a crusade against everything that was phony, pretentious, or untrue, and moreover, it established a standard of excellence that turned out to be enduring."[14]

This standard was set for the American stage with *What Price Glory?* — produced in 1924 and co-authored by Stallings and Maxwell Anderson, another *World* writer, who, captivated by Stallings' war reminiscences, talked Stallings into collaborating on the play. An instant success on the stage in 1924, this production led to additional collaboration: their *First Flight* and *The Buccaneer* were produced in 1925. Meanwhile, however, Stallings' novel *Plumes* had been published in 1924. Stallings was suddenly famous, and Hollywood wanted him.

Irving Thalberg, who was to become the "subject of F. Scott Fitzgerald's *The Last Tycoon*,"[15] took Stallings to Hollywood and introduced him to King Vidor who, tired of "ephemeral films . . . wanted a story of a young American who was neither over-patriotic or [sic] a pacifist, but who went to war and reacted normally to all the things that happened to him."[16] Stallings took with him a short story, "The Big Parade," and Vidor found it to be what he wanted; but getting Stallings to work was another matter. As Vidor explained, "Stallings was too exhilerated by the battle of Hollywood to settle down. With a play in New York garnering high praise and high box-office receipts, with his first effort at a screenplay sold to M-G-M, Stallings couldn't picture himself in a studio cubicle, grinding out a scenario for a war movie."[17]

When Stallings announced that he was returning to New York, Vidor followed him in order to keep him talking about "The Big Parade." Stallings spent the return trip reminiscing about the war, and Vidor was "overwhelmed" by Stallings' stories which seemed "too fantastic and unreal" until one night, while he was sitting in his lower berth, "the train started a violent swaying action." Vidor described what happened next: "Stallings' wooden leg, hanging on a wall hook, swung in a wide arc with the motion of the train and the heavy brogue on the wooden foot kicked me hard in the chin. When I recovered from the blow, the evidence of the swaying leg with the sock and shoe still on it was all too real. I could never again say to myself that the horrors of war didn't happen; I accepted the facts."[18]

In New York, Stallings was too busy with publishing houses, theater conferences, and cocktail parties to spend time with Vidor; but the movie director trailed Stallings until the script was completed. According to Vidor, the movie *The Big Parade* was so successful that it ran on Broadway for two years; made Vidor famous as a director; won stardom for its lead, John Gilbert; and helped establish Metro-Goldwyn-Mayer financially. From that time on, Stallings was a writer welcome in Hollywood although it was difficult to pin down the impatient young author for any length of time.

V *In North Carolina*

By 1926, Stallings was ready to "retire" from the New York *World* and to settle in a renovated farmhouse (which was given to the young couple by Dr. William Louis Poteat) in what is now Blanch, North Carolina, which is fifteen miles from Danville, Virginia. The young Stallings spent the summer adding a wing which was to be (and still is) Stallings' library. Among the many impressive facsimiles which Stallings collected are numerous books which he reviewed for the *World*, as well as the complete works of his favorite authors such as Shakespeare, G. B. Shaw, Honoré de Balzac, and Joseph Conrad. Few markings appear, however, except in Shaw's Preface to *Heartbreak House* where Stallings invariably underlined war commentary with which he completely agreed. But Stallings wrote so much from personal experience, with such a basic honesty, that it is impossible to determine specific literary influences except through occasional and obvious allusions, such as those quoted throughout this study.

Stallings settled only briefly in North Carolina. He tried his hand at gentleman farming but continued writing — specifically, short stories. By 1928, the restless young author had returned to New York to collaborate with Oscar Hammerstein, II, on the musical, *Rainbow*, produced that year and filmed in 1930 as *Song of the West*. In 1928 the Stallings' first child, Sylvia, was born — the second, Diana, was born in 1932 — but the family spent little time in their renovated "Forest Home." Stallings maintained an apartment in New York where he and his family lived together until the mid 1930's, but they journeyed to "Forest Home" for their summers and for special holidays. They lived lavishly for a time, and Stallings began to gamble and drink more heavily as he adapted none too well to his sudden fame and fortune.[19]

VI *Out of Retirement*

Tired of retirement by 1931, Stallings began to write for the New York *Sun* where he published approximately four hundred long literary articles in which he reviewed, as he had for the *World*, books in every area of knowledge. Meantime, he had met Ernest Hemingway and adapted for the stage — and in 1932 for the screen — Hemingway's *A Farewell to Arms*. At the same time, he was publishing short stories and working on *The First World War: A Pictorial History* for Simon and Schuster (1933); but he was increasingly reluctant to write. In his second introduction to *The First World War*, reissued in 1962, Stallings wrote that he had no conscious desire to prepare that book. But, quite like King Vidor, Lincoln Schuster followed Stallings — this time to Hollywood — where Schuster was at Stallings' house every day until he "had written every caption, and a preface, along the original plan" that Stallings had first outlined. The book was immediately successful.

Stallings' editorial work — as well as his newspaper experience, his fame and general literary abilities — led to other offers. In 1934, he became editor of Fox Movietonews; and, in 1935, he became literary editor of the *American Mercury*. He was replaced in 1936 by his friend, Captain J. W. Thomason, Jr., when, in October, Stallings became associate editor — serving until May, 1937. His vast knowledge of history and of books in general is reflected particularly in the "Library" section of that magazine.

More exciting adventures occurred during the same period, and in August, 1935, sponsored by Fox Movietonews and the North American Newspaper Alliance, Stallings left America to lead a news and newsreel expedition to Ethiopia to cover the expected Italian attack; as a result, his newsreel coverage and his newspaper releases appeared throughout the country for the remainder of the year. Stallings returned to the United States by February, 1936. Now estranged from his wife, he asked for a divorce; and, on October 20, his wife established residence in Reno. The divorce was granted December 1, 1936, and according to her, their mutual friend, Walter Lippmann, became the guardian of their children.

Almost three months later, on Valentine's Day, Stallings' engagement to his young secretary at Fox, Louise St. Leger Vance, was announced. Married on March 19, 1937, they left for an eight-week honeymoon in Europe as Stallings began his "second life." After their return, Stallings signed a contract with Metro-Goldwyn-Mayer as a screen writer; the couple moved to Santa Barbara, California; and there, his first son, Laurence, Jr., was born on March 6, 1939. In Hollywood, he worked on such films as *Too Hot to Handle* (1938) and *Northwest Passage* (1940); but, according to the second Mrs. Laurence Stallings, he thought little of cinematic work and "did not like to write for the films."[20] Stallings had long felt that motion pictures tended to oversimplify most of the ills of the world. Furthermore, he felt that the early movies omitted too much that was real in life; and he said so in "Celluloid Psychology."[21] Nonetheless, the movies provided additional income; and by then he needed it.

On September 5, 1941, Stallings' fourth and last child, Sally (now Mrs. Edward Bland Potter of Fresno, California) was born. Seven months later, on April 2, 1942, Stallings returned to active military duty, going immediately to Washington, D.C. There he was, for much of the time, stationed at the Pentagon; but he also spent some time in Africa, Europe, and England. Robert Lovett, then Assistant Secretary of War, described Stallings' World War II duties in this way: "He was substantially used as an advisor by the Services, particularly by his own service, in the field of public relations and in interviewing troops at various stations to check on their equipment and their gripes."[22] But Arthur Krock is certain that Stallings was "engaged in Army and Marine Intelligence work," so much so that he barely saw him during this period. Krock, at the time Washington correspondent for the New York *Times*, knew that Stallings was avoiding him: "It was so obvious that he had to."[23] But in a letter to Krock in 1962 in which Stallings sought Krock's assistance in securing military photographs for *The Doughboys*, Stallings briefly summarized his World War II experience: "I was a Marine officer on Headquarters Staff of General Henry H. Arnold (Chief of Interview Section, War Room). Thus I am familiar with the men and weapons of the National Guard, the Regular Army, and the Staff. . . . "[24] (Stallings means that *he* was Interview chief: General Arnold, of course, was commander of the Army Air Forces.)

While I have no access to Stallings' war record, classified or unclassified, his stories of such notables as Anthony Eden and Winston Churchill, who are often referred to in the Stallings-Krock correspondence (now at the Firestone Library, Princeton University), suggest that Stallings' role in World War II was more than that of interviewing American troops. For example, in a letter dated October 26, 1962, he shares what he calls a "note on Intelligence at the highest level"; and he occasionally scribbles "This is classified" beside an anecdote he shares. The Stallings-Krock correspondence also reflects Stallings' continued interest in games, words, and world leaders, as well as his ideas for future works, such as "an anthology of Churchill's epigrams and loudly spoken asides."[25]

After Stallings retired with the rank of lieutanant-colonel on June 27, 1943, the family settled in Whittier, California. Though officially retired, Stallings went to Hollywood to assist old friends, such as King Vidor (A Miracle Can Happen, 1948) and Merian C. Cooper (She Wore a Yellow Ribbon, 1949).[26] He wrote one play, The Streets Are Guarded, based on World War II. Produced in 1944, the play, unpublished, closed after twenty-four performances though Burns Mantle wrote that it deserved a much better reception.[27] Much of his time in later years was devoted to continued writing and reading and watching football games, but Stallings published no new fiction after 1932. According to his wife, however, he did write other short stories, and worked off and on at another novel, which he never completed.[28] Finally, in 1959, he published "The War to End War," and Max Wyeth of Harper and Row urged him to expand it to book length. No such book treatment of World War I existed; it was needed, and Stallings was the man to write it. At the age of sixty-five, Stallings entered into three years of research for this work which was published in 1963 as The Doughboys.

That same year Stallings' second leg was amputated because of wounds suffered during the first war and because of the many falls to which he was prone because of his artificial leg. The next year, through arrangements initiated by Arthur Krock and Congressman Carl Vinson of Georgia, Stallings, on June 24, 1964, was honored for his contribution and his service to his country. That honor was presented by Major General Raymond Kier, Fleet Marine Commander, who, "with a full complement of officers and men" delivered to Stallings' home a "shadow box, complete with miniature decorations, USMC emblems and silver plaque."[29] Four years later, Stallings who had finally decided to complete the unfinished novel, became ill and, at the age of seventy-three, died of a heart attack, February 29, 1968, at his home in the Pacific Palisades. His remains are buried in Rosecrans Veterans' Cemetery, Point Loma, California.

VII *Opinions*

Most often described by those who knew him as a brilliant man with a vast store of knowledge, as an excellent conversationalist, or as a man with an exceptional memory and a great sense of humor, Stallings was always fascinated by games (a continuing motif in his works), especially those involving high competiton and risks. Roland Neel recalled Stallings' telling him of being invited by a prominent New York family to a gambling party at the Biltmore Hotel in New York; "He said he threw the dice for $10,000 — just one roll. He didn't say if he won or lost. He was more fascinated by the challenge and the risk." His friend King Vidor, who compared him to Ernest Hemingway, described them as "similar in their desire to accent or emphasize their virility and manhood."[30] Surely each writer sought dangerous adventure throughout his life, and both drew on experience for successful writing in several forms. Both suffered from the war physically and psychologically, though Stallings' personal loss was much greater. And each responded in the novel form with disillusionment about the war, just as each, in his own way, had to cope with a war-created trauma in readjusting to life. Stallings' disillusionment is more understandable as rebellion against war and its causes, since he retained his faith in man and in his country.

He seems to have found much solace in story telling, particularly in stories about the Civil War, which was always his favorite topic. And, despite almost continual pain, Stallings managed to retain a sense of humor. Evelyn and Roland Neel recalled that when they visited him two weeks before he died, he was propped up on a "specially made bed, a blue French beret cocked on the side of his head, laughing and telling tales. He was always entertaining."[31]

But underlying what Evelyn Neel would agree was "a bold front" was another aspect of Stallings' personality. She explained: "Ever since I can remember there was always a bitterness about Laurence. I never knew anyone who just pulled down everything and never gave you anything to replace it. He was an iconoclast. That's exactly my impression of him — though the last time I saw him he seemed to have mellowed some." His wife, however, in a letter to me described him as "a modest man, a good marine. He was so patriotic; he loved his country so much."

Stallings was apparently "different to different people" as Paul Green, dramatist, has expressed it.[32] Generally, friends and contemporaries seem to have admired his personal bravery as much as his literary talent. According to Lowell Thomas, a working contemporary at Twentieth Century Fox during the 1930's, Stallings was regarded there "as an unusually talented person" with "tremendous energy and great charm," who "despite constant pain never mentioned it."[33] And James M. Cain, the novelist, echoed similar sentiments about his "incredible bravery." Cain illustrated this courage with a story of the "decent, gallant and in all ways admirable" Stallings who refused to allow Cain, right "out of the TB hospital," to carry a can of gasoline when their automobile ran out of gas on a Sunday drive to Arthur Krock's. Cain realized what "stumping on foot" for several blocks meant to Stallings, but Stallings persisted with "You're just a goddam war cripple, that's all." Cain added that, with the remark, Stallings "cut loose with his sardonic laugh, which had to be heard to be believed"; and Cain concluded that Stallings' own attitude toward his leg was "sardonic": "There was a streak in his nature that simply would not claim credit or be heroic, or anything of that kind. Also, I think it helped to be able to pretend occasionally that someone was a worse war cripple than he was."[34]

To Cain, however, it was Stallings' "military side" that "emotionally satisfied" him "as nothing else did." But Cain felt that *What Price Glory?* with its "tremendous success . . . put Stallings on a track he should never have run on, or tried to run on" since he lacked the talent "to deliver."[35] Stallings' first wife, Helen, would agree about *What Price Glory?* — but for a different reason. She felt that success came too quick and easily for Stallings and that it spoiled him. Their mutual friend King Vidor agreed partially with that conclusion; but he thinks that Stallings' "ebullient nature," his "love of life," made him restless and difficult "to pin down, to keep . . . interested in any one project for very long."[36] Furthermore, Vidor believed that Stallings "had an unconscious guilt complex which made him feel he had to suffer, or have something *cut* from his physical body in recompense."

That Ernest Hemingway not only anthologized "Vale of Tears" in *Men at War* but retained the story in the 1955 reissue is evidence of a contemporary's respect for him as a writer. And letters in which Sherwood Anderson sought collaboration with Stallings reflect his respect for Stallings the dramatist.[37] But Stallings thought little of his own literary accomplishments — except for *The Doughboys* — and in his later years concluded that "the fictioneer had no great truth to offer." He turned, instead, to the works of "Scientific Humanists" because, in his own words, "They are the only writers who make no pretenses of not knowing."[38]

His lifelong pursuit of truth was, in part, influenced by his psychological reaction to his wound and by an attempt to understand his own history, and hence reconcile himself to it. A man who seems to have lived two lives — with two wives and two families — and a veteran of two wars who lost two legs, Laurence Stallings was both an enigmatic man and a writer who tried to sever himself from his past by returning to it in his writing. It is curious, for example, that Stallings never saw his first family after he re-married. He gave up all of his property, including his rather large and impressive library which contained such rare manuscripts as a Shakespeare First Folio.[39] He broke off relationships with many friends he and his wife had shared. And he never returned to his birthplace of Macon. When he died in 1968, he was a forgotten man in his native state of Georgia. The obituary — primarily from an Associated Press release — which appeared in the Atlanta *Journal* on March 1, 1968, began: "The death of Laurence Stallings was hardly noticed in Georgia where he was born 73 years ago, but at one time Stallings was a man to consider in the American literary scene." The obituary in the *Macon Telegraph and News* was largely taken from the same press release, but a few comments by Roland Neel were added. The local paper has no file on Stallings — nor do the local libraries, the Washington Memorial Library, or the Mercer University Library. In New York City, however, his death rated a full two-column review of his life and career, which reads in part: " . . . he was known to acquaintances as genial and friendly . . . [he] read with lightning speed and had a prodigious memory. He was said to have possessed an uncanny talent for getting into barroom fights and losing them — and an equally uncanny talent for making friends of celebrated people. . . . He had not let the experiences of war embitter or disillusion him. . . . War was Mr. Stallings' theme — and he approached it with a hard line."[40]

CHAPTER 2

Disillusionment: Plumes

PLUMES, an autobiographical novel, reflects the impact of war and the rebellion of the period following it. Portions of the novel are set at Woodland College, which was really Wake Forest. Stallings and Helen Poteat are the prototypes of young Richard and Esme, the two central characters.

I *Structure, Plot, Characterization, Setting*

The novel is divided into five books. Their titles, as well as the poetic epigraphs which introduce each chapter, define the content of each book. Book One, "Battered Plumes," includes four chapters which trace the ancestry of the Plumes, their culture, their educational background, and their invariable military experiences. The hero, Richard Plume, is linked to the long, essentially patriotic and martial family tradition; and the reader sees the protagonist as he entrains for, and returns from, the war.

The epigraph for Chapter I is taken from Thomas Campbell's "Stanzas to the Memory of Spanish Patriots," 1843: "Long trains of ill pass unheeded, dumb/ But vengeance is behind and justice is to come." We might interpret these lines literally in relation to the author who, in *Plumes*, begins his crusade to tell the truth about war. However, in relation to his protagonist as we see him in Chapter I, the quotation suggests something of the young warrior's enthusiasm (naiveté) before the battle. Since everything that occurs in the novel is set in Book One, a close explication of it is necessary. Ironically, the novel begins at its chronological conclusion in 1922 after the Harding inaugural with Richard's comment that, of those Plumes living in this country for two hundred and fifty years, not one was ever worth twenty-five thousand dollars, nor "had anything worth going to war about."[1] He adds, however, that "not one of them failed to be in *the first wave*" of any war.

In a flashback, the reader has his first glimpse of the young warrior Richard, a Marine "dousing his body before entraining for the Advanced Zone." His physique is described as "a beautiful thing. . . ." He has the "shoulders of a Rodin mold, with a shock of burnished hair topping a wild, happy face."² He pounds his chest "in an ecstasy of watery thrills, for the air of Paris is lively in May, and his cavernous torso gave off a thumping sound as if it had been a Tartar war-drum." Nearby, members of his platoon skirmish with "Senegalese casuals"; and, as Plume dashes to their rescue, a military policeman, Captain Whiting, arrives to untangle "the lozenged mass."³ Plume later introduces himself to Whiting, and the two part with Plume's "I hope I'll meet you again."⁴ The chapter closes with nearby spectators admiring the naked Plume who runs "like Daphne" as charwomen shout, ". . . *vous êtes plus grand.*"⁵

In Chapter II, the action shifts to 1685 and a history of the Plumes. The first, Jabez, "rested on his oars," having married a rich planter's daughter who owned three thousand acres of land, of which 2980 were covered with "magnificent standing timber."⁶ Jabez, who is described as the "daddy of them all," came to this country because so many others did too. Thus the Plumes' beginnings are equated with doing the popular thing which is not particularly associated with any noble ideal, but Jabez begins the tradition which passes down through every generation. Jabez left his son Christian nothing. Christian ". . . multiplied before the Lord, his wife being the sum of Noah, Jesse, Patience and Charity":

Of these, Noah concerns the present Richard more than the others, for Noah had his fine red shock torn from him by an Indian, but only after he had duplicated his body in the person of another Noah. It is said that the first Noah Plume was killed while on a scouting patrol organized by an unfortified settlement. He thus founded the war-like tradition, persisted in unto this day among the Plumes, of going to war to save your neighbor's property.⁷

The second Noah Plume lost seven toes in the Revolution "while making America Safe for Democracy." But his wound actually resulted from his encountering the enemy while out to "shoot rabbits for provender and for moccasins. . . ."⁸ When Noah returned home, he "founded a tradition" when his youngest son asked, "Did it hurt, pappy?", and he responded, "'Naw' . . . drenching his descendants in blood."⁹ This question and much the same answer are repeated again at the center of the novel and at the end.

Noah's son, George Washington Plume, fought Indians "in the Creek Wars in Georgia" and returned "to christen his fourth child Old Hickory Plume"[10] after General Andrew Jackson — solely because Jackson had given Plume a toddy from "his personal demijohn, in order to nerve the sergeant when the hot irons were applied to his amputation."[11] Old Hickory, Richard's grandfather, fought at Buena Vista in the Mexican War and returned with a stump arm. He was the first to refuse to "sit in a chimney corner and lick his wounds in silent penury" — thereby founding another tradition. He amassed a considerable fortune ($20,000) which included land and buildings, but they were unfortunately located to the northwest of Marthasville, Georgia, which "later became the City of Atlanta" and the site of Sherman's "pass."[12] Old Hickory survived the Civil War but met his absurd death through a boast, passed on by ex-slave Toby "who had not sat at Old Hickory's feet for nothing."[13] Toby said that "Marse Hick" could "whup all de white trash in the Konfeddit States of Merikky wid dat one arm tie behind his back." When hooded ruffians later arrived, "Marse Hick failed to meet Toby's accounts of his prowess."[14]

Old Hickory's son, Zachary Taylor Plume (Richard's father), "delighted in pomp as a Persian"[15] but had to wait fifteen years longer than usual before he knew "the choking pride of the dress parade, and the sharp barks of a platoon leader . . ." in the Spanish-American War. Zachary kept an album and would later "secretly thrill at his own martial picture." He liked to show it to his wife, Penelope, for "it brought her gusts of memory — of a tall young man, Bayard of a southern town — who strode in his volunteer captain's uniform. . . ."[16] His favorite reading was Froissart's *Chronicles*, and he named his son Richard Coeur de Lion Plume[17] because his wife's labor pains began ". . . just at the moment that Zachary was summing up the chronicler in respect to the Plantaganets: 'Whatever may have been their faults . . . there was not a coward among them.' "[18]

His son Richard, who grew up on "first hand instruction in martial history . . .," delighted in Confederate Memorial Day parades where, as a boy, he struggled "frantically for the brass shells of the saluting rifles." Not until a boyhood trip to New York does he learn from a friend that "Grant beat Robert E. Lee !," and "the boy . . . had sown the seeds of disillusion. Tactical walks gave way to botanizing before the next winter, and no more divisions were swept away. History had been untrue."[19] The action then shifts in Chapter

III to Woodland College in 1912 where Richard is studying the classics and biology, which are taught by Dr. Quintus Horatius Dozier and Dr. John Milton Bibb, respectively.[20] Richard is also attracted to football "for glory"[21] and to Dr. Dozier's daughter, Esme, niece of Dr. Bibb.

The first knowledge which Esme receives from her uncle concerning Richard is that "his father's military history classes had convinced him that science is the only thing to teach, because it's the only thing a man can know."[22] Not until Richard's sophomore year do Esme and Richard get to know each other better. Richard comes to Dr. Bibb's house with biological specimens and finds the two leaning over a spider's nest. As they watch the male spider advancing in "a series of concentric circles . . . towards his lady," making the most of "his decorations, waving and gesticulating with the arm bands," both Richard and Esme are fascinated: "The Black Knight of the arm bands moved a millimeter closer to the [sic] belle dame sans merci . . . . The knight's body fell headless at the postern. The lady prepared to withdraw him into her castle."[23]

Following this scene is a discussion of football, a game which Esme opposes and which Richard loves: "There's such a challenge to play. Each week you go to some big college. You come out on the field in ragged blankets and old helmets, and they almost jeer you. They prepare to run over you. Then they find they can't. There's a savage pleasure in surprising them. They send in their best men . . . . You know you will lose . . . . You discard all those illusions and simply stand and fight. It's pure fighting instinct from then on . . . it almost seems a struggle for survival."[24]

After listening to Richard, Esme concludes that Richard will never be "a biologist . . . . I suppose you will tell your students that the War in Europe is the highest expression of man . . . .[25] The survival of the fittest means a survival of the best adapted within a species. You can't go through life . . . swinging your fists one minute and being civilized the next." But Richard "succumbed to temptation" and again went out for football, hoping that, when he next saw Esme, "she would admire him for something in him which made him helpless before the call of football."[26] As he approaches her, she notices "the white arm bands of his sweater oscillating slowly"; and she calls, "Spider, spider . . . Shall I bite off your head?"[27]

Chapter IV includes the goodbye ceremony for Richard, now married, who is cited as "a great example" as he embarks on the war crusade ("They were singing 'Onward Christian Soldiers' and

Richard was almost running as he moved up the aisle.")[28] The latter part of this brief chapter,[29] the concluding one of Book One, tells of Richard's return and of Esme's joining him at a hospital in New Jersey in April, 1919. There is a brief description of the happiness of the nation — "an era of good feeling," attributed to the economy — and Esme notes the chivalrous behavior of the "country throbbing with a victorious wave of hysterical patriotism."[30] Everyone is unusually kind to her and her baby as she travels to their wounded Marine.

As Richard and Esme are reunited, Stallings writes: "Richard Plume felt the cheek against his. He was weak, and the odor of her skin so buoyant his pulse jumped as though he were a gas patient under an oxygen bell. Every wound in his body, and there were seven, was painted with a cool liquid fire. He could have cried out with the anguished happiness of the contact from his cheek. For six months he had lain thus . . . sane and insane, awaiting this consummation."[31] When Plume's bony arms "circled her . . .," they "clung thus and went shares in sufferings" while Plume prayerfully responded, "God forgive me for my folly."[32]

Action is foreshadowed by the chapter's opening epigraph from Charles Kingsley's "Young and Old" (1862): "Creep home to take your place there / The spent and maimed among / God grant you find a face there / You loved when all was young." Significantly, the chapter centers on views of the young and old with Esme's and Richard's visit to Woodland where Dean Baylor, Dr. Dozier, Dr. Bibb, and Richard's parents beg him to return, and offer sympathy which Richard scorns. Dean Baylor says, "It was God's own mercy that saved him, and down here we think it was for a life of further service to the Christian ideal." Dr. Dozier tells Esme: "He'll come home. Who ever heard of an old soldier who didn't creep home to old friends and romance about his wounds?"

The four remaining books of *Plumes* can be treated more briefly since the work includes many repetitions revealed through speech, actions, and recollections by the characters. Book Two, "The Shorn Helm," is primarily the story of the wounded hero's struggle to adjust to civilian life as he searches for a job while Esme looks for a home so that son Dickie can join them in Washington, D.C. Esme prefers returning to Woodland where Plume has been offered an instructorship in biology, but Plume is determined: "Before I creep home for good I'm going to find out why this thing happened to me and see to it that you [Dickie] will keep those two little kneecaps of yours all through your life."[33]

The decision to remain in Washington leads to difficulties for the Plumes who cannot afford the high rent, which is attributed to the change to President Harding from President Wilson. "Winning politicians promising to enter the League of Nations, and also open the treasury doors to the yapping heroes, descended upon Washington . . . seeking remunerative work for blood-kin. . . ."[34] This situation adds to Richard's difficulty in finding a job, for former government employees "were reluctant to be driven from Eden to the outer darkness of provincial towns." Richard is finally hired by the "Chief of the Research Division,"[35] and there he meets Mr. Gary, another wounded veteran whose "face . . . might have worn a crown of thorns." Gary tells Richard: "Christ, but I'm glad you're the new man. . . . Other fellow was patriotic. Got on my nerves."[36]

While Richard is buying yellow blossoms for Esme who awaits the news of his venture, she reads from a book, *The Story of My Heart*,[37] Richard's underlined passage: "In human affairs everything happens by chance — that is, in defiance of human ideals, and without any direction of an intelligence. A man bathes in a pool; a crocodile seizes and lacerates his flesh. If any one maintains that an intelligence directed that cruelty. . . ."[38] This passage foreshadows Richard's tendencies toward more naturalistic concepts, a development counterpointed by Esme who grows more romantic throughout the novel.

Richard's interest in science continues as he persists in rejecting the teaching position at Woodland; for he and Gary, who have become friends, share an interest in science. Richard tells Gary that war is " . . . a brutal and vicious dance directed by ghastly men."[39] But he remembers a time when " . . . there was a spirit America had never known before, a willingness to look at life in terms of humanity and not of imaginary geographical lines." Gary insists that "Truth lies at the bottom of a microscope. The sooner you realize that all of your suffering comes to exactly the same thing that might have been gained from a fall under a freight train . . . the sooner you'll find some degree of mental rest. It will save you from the delusion of service in the sense of crusading."[40] Plume can admit that the war was absurd for both sides as he recalls shooting a German boy "who had been fed exactly the same diet of shining swords . . ."[41]; and he concludes, "It's so absurd that I cannot discuss it."[42]

Appropriately, this chapter's epigraph is taken from William Blake's poem "The Tiger" (1793): "What immortal hand or eye / Could frame thy fearful symmetry?" Directly related to the many oppositions inherent in attitudes expressed toward war and life, the epigraph serves to define the irreconcilable dilemma that is seemingly expressed: Can anything worthwhile (beautiful or good) result from so terrible an experience; how can there be a God directing these cruelties? The mysterious fascination and repulsion of war, treated in this, the longest chapter of the novel, stresses the absurdity of life which is filled with contradictions. By the end of Book Two, and halfway through the novel, the Plumes "seemed more battered than ever. . . . "[43] This statement answers the question contained in the epigraph of Chapter VII, from William Collins' "Ode" (1746), "How sleep the brave who sink to rest / By all their Country's wishes blest. . . ."

Richard encourages Esme to divorce him, but she is determined to stay with him. Plume begins to see himself as "a monster,"[44] but he cannot change because of an "unquenchable anger" at himself and the "ignorance that victimized" him. As Book Two closes, the Plumes have finally rented an apartment and settled in Washington. Gary tells the hero: " 'If you are smashed badly . . . and if you have any intelligence . . . you must remake a world to live in' — he seemed labored to state it — 'if you can accept war, go home and be your sunny old man with your hickory stick.' "[45]

The center book, "The Caitiff Knight," is especially important in that, structurally, all that occurs in the remaining two books is foreshadowed in it. This third book includes two excursions within the city of Washington: the Plumes sally forth (1) to the inaugural parade, and (2) to see the play *Hamlet*. As Book Three opens (Chapter VIII), it soon becomes apparent that the literal romance between Esme and Richard has waned considerably. Stallings summarizes their dilemma in Shakespearean phraseology: "For him the time was out of joint. For her the setting." Numerous reversals begin to take place in the second half of the novel, for Richard grows more realistic; Esme, more romantic. Richard is more determined in his efforts; Esme, more dramatic, is retrogressing to her girlish ideals as she finally decides that life "is hopeless."[46] She longs for "woods and sleepy towns," not "factories and cities."[47] She begins to wish that "the South had been permitted to secede" from the Union.[48] She is increasingly convinced of Richard's madness: " 'You can't be sane in the midst of our life' — she waved about the room — 'in all of this, unless fed by some inner fire. Something not of this earth or earthly. . . . "[49] Richard, who responds in a long and moving passage, will not accept the possibility of spiritual growth. He equates "spirit" with a "long line of Baptist preachers" threatening him with "the horror of death":

I was to be interested in another life. I've lost that interest, and I'm not afraid to die. Three times I had blood transfusions . . . was dead before they were given me, and nothing had come of it. I can walk into a church with its promises of peace hereafter and its scorn to consider this present room . . . and laugh into a preacher's face. I have died. What does he know about death? He'll tell me how Christ died to save me. . . . I did the same thing and voluntarily. . . . A foolish little Christ all over again. . . . And after all, the man of Nazareth had only three hours upon a cross. I've had hundreds. How many expiations must there be before I can approach death with serenity? From now on, for me, all things are as they seem, and nothing more.[50]

On a visit to Mount Vernon, Esme runs about the lawn and admires the home as representative of a beautiful way of life that has been destroyed: "She waved towards slave quarters, kitchen gardens, stables . . . with a circling gesture. 'If we could all return to this sort of life we would all be happy.' "[51] Gary and Richard discuss war while Esme looks through the house, and Richard concludes that the Revolution " . . . was the only war ever worth while."[52]

The trip on March 14, 1921, to the inaugural parade is made to please Esme who wants to see Woodrow Wilson: "Wilson was a great man; next to Jesus Christ, the Son of God, he had best impressed the ideals of human brotherhood into permanent literary form."[53] But Richard's interest in Wilson is that of one cripple looking at another as Wilson drags his leg while leaving the parade. Richard explains: "He thinks he's the only man who really was deeply disappointed in this hellish mess. It was all his crusade. None other's. . . . He thinks no one else hobbles as badly. I suffered for him just now. He was ashamed."[54] Both Wilson and Plume are described as "knights with shorn-helms, withheld from the tourneys of the world" as Stallings gives what appears to be an eye-witness report of an event which took place during those years in which he lived in Washington.

The novel builds to a climax as Esme and Richard attend the play *Hamlet,* after which Richard falls on ice and injures his knee. Repelled by Esme's sympathy, and taking his cue from Hamlet, "He waved her away violently": he shouted "We must quit. Please get out of my sight. I don't love you. Something's torn that out of me. I don't want you. I've no right to you!"[55] As a police patrol speeds Richard to Walter Reed Hospital, he recalls, for the only time in the novel, his battlefield wound:

He surveyed his legs in wonderment. The right kneecap was still glistening white, despite the low light from the west, as it hung by its ligaments over the jagged opening of his stained breeches. Shock terrific. Who thought shock so terrific? That damned musketry school at Gondrecourt. . . . Why, by God, this was no play-school. . . . This was it . . . and it had got him. Who cared about Belgium and the Lusitania? To hell with the Lusitania. Richard Plume, center of the universe, had life stolen from him. Stolen . . . by all those scoundrels who were not there upon the ground with him. The God-damned scoundrelly orators were not there. . . .
      Parades and parades and parades. Esme. He had given her up. . . . Would she know he died with his head up? Three of them gone to hell and will return. The second coming. Would she ever know he was dead? . . . Sweater stuck on root pull it off Esme made it. Oh, God, how bloody tail is now they'll find him and let darling Esme know so heavenly and he gave up for this and was cheated out of his heart for no use. . . . Ought to have guides on battlefields to pilot wounded men who got grip enough to crawl to Esme. If there was a guide. "Where's heavenly guide you God-damned Jehovah of an Israelite tyrant?"[56]

He lapses deeper into unconsciousness; and Stallings, in the stream-of-consciousness style, writes: "Langsam langsam langsam you German you German flatheads keep that right end up, keep it up keepitupkeepitup keepitup langsam langsamlangsam million-sixtyeleven tons of Esme . . . Morphia mon medicin morphia beacoupdemorphia s'il vous plait excrivez monsieur au madame Richard Plume. . . ."[57] As Book Three closes and Esme is saying good-bye in the hospital to Richard, he is again begging forgiveness, "Try to forgive me . . ."[58]
      "Tourneys" is the title of Book Four, and it appropriately includes several "attacks."[59] Richard is out of the hospital and is working for Mr. Meyer who publishes *The Wounded Doughboy*.[60] Richard's first "attack" is on the Veteran's Administration where he takes a young veteran who has been unable to collect any compensation for his wound. His second attack is at Tom Paine Hall where he and Gary attend a meeting with Mr. Meyer who is working for the release of jailed conscientious objectors. Mr. Meyer convinces Gary to speak; but, as he begins, four veterans in the rear of the audience begin to sing "My Country 'Tis of Thee." Richard, enraged, strikes full force at the mouths of the men, and falls in the act — an act which even-

tually leads to amputation of his leg. Captain Whiting (the military policeman from Chapter I) is one of the four hecklers. Recalling that the hall resembled the Woodland chapel just before he went to war, Plume thinks: "Fools like this kept me from ever knowing the truth."[61] Gary had warned Meyer before they went: "Don't trust Plume down there among men who refuse to fight. All this present phase of his will pass and he will revert to a man with a helmet and a sword. I shouldn't wonder if he'd revert as soon as he heard his country damned. He's a patriot."[62] But Richard's action was the result of what he considered an insult to his friend Gary.

The above passage is paralleled by an episode in Shakespeare's *Troilus and Cressida* from which the chapter's epigraph is taken: "The baby figure of the giant mass / That is to come at large." In Shakespeare, these lines are spoken by the Greek commander Nestor who suggested that Achilles accept Hector's challenge to single combat, but Ulysses convinces Nestor that Ajax would be a better challenger: "Ajax employ'd plucks down Achilles' plumes" (I.iii.386). Ajax, however, is actually Hector's own nephew; and, when the two meet in battle, Hector cannot fight against his own blood-kin.

The final chapter of Book Four ("Tourneys") includes the literal attack at Tom Paine Hall; and the book ends with Richard's fainting from the pain of his fall.[63] The fifth and last book, "Battered Plumes," includes only one chapter as the novel moves to a hasty conclusion.[64] Richard's mother, Penelope, comes to patch up the marriage of Richard and Esme; she tells him that divorce "would be a stigma."[65] Fourth-cousin Jabez of the War Department offers Richard a job; and Esme returns to her wounded knight to take him back to Woodland. Richard's leg has been amputated, and Penelope hopes that "with the loss of the leg had gone the discontent, and the poison it had been secreting into his blood-stream." She says, "You are a Child of the King. You are resting in the Everlasting Arms."[66] Richard replies, "That's the cruellest superstition," and is reluctant to return to Woodland: "I don't know what to do. . . . There are so many things I'd like to smash . . . that I can never even make a dent in. There's an Arms Conference in two weeks. They are going to bury the Unknown Soldier, and then talk of ending the war. People such as you [Esme] and I never will revenge ourselves if we go home. War will come again!"[67]

He decides what to do during a visit to the site of the Unknown Soldier's grave, the day before burial. Another funeral is in progress,

and he sees his son Dickie "grasping about the green sward, collecting the empty brass shells"[68] just as he had done during his own
youth. Determined to break the pattern of history, he agrees to
return to Woodland and to the biology instructorship. The novel
ends with a conversation between Gary and Dickie that burns with
understatement — revealing the senseless emotionalism which had
spurred the country's patriotic wave five years earlier but had
transcended all wars and all time. Dickie asks Gary:

> "What's a grave for?"
> "For a soldier to sleep in."
> "Why doesn't he sleep in his bed?"
> "Generals won't let him," Gary said solemnly.
> "What's a general?"
> "A man . . . who makes little boys sleep in graves."

II   *Imagery, Symbolism, Theme*

As far as Richard's crusade is concerned, the return to Woodland
means defeat. Earlier he had told Esme: "We have been wronged.
We may endure it by returning to Woodland, but we can never right
it."[69] In the end, Plume appears to accept endurance only out of ac-
commodation to his wife and son. Richard seems to have no concern
for rebirth, although the setting of Woodland, and the time, spring,
would suggest this symbolically. His act is one of self-sacrifice —
punishment for the guilt-ridden man who has brought only unhap-
piness to his family.

Plumes, a novel of artistic symmetry, revolves around repeated
beginnings and endings, quests and attacks, as history repeats itself
throughout each generation. The dominant motifs of war and
romance are linked through action, character, imagery, and setting.
Yet the novel is complex. Embodied in Stallings' treatment of each
of these motifs are numerous contradictions inherent not only in war
and in romance but in life itself. These contradictions may be viewed
as a series of polarities which lead to reversals in attitudes as well as
in actions. For example, the romance of war which at first appeals to
Richard also eventually leads to his crusade to tell the truth — and
his truth is directly related to science which lays bare untested concepts.

In relation to each of the motifs, there is rejection and acceptance,
hell and peace, the Fall and Eden, a denial of God and an equation
with Christ. There are the parades of war and politics, but there are
also the pomp and show in everyday life — even in football games.

There are pacifism and patriotism, bad and sweet smells, shrill sounds and whispers, city and country, age and youth, immobility and mobility — and all are in some way linked with romance, war, and life. Though war is always in the background of the novel, a greater war exists in the mind and in everyday psychological adjustment to existence, an existence which seems largely determined by economics (property). Irony is heaped on irony throughout the novel when it deals with the economics which literally affected each generation of Plumes and linked each directly with a war of economic origin. Paradoxically, war deprived them of limbs with which to work for the country for which they fought.

The whole concept of chivalry and courtly love — still so much a living tradition, particularly in the deep South — becomes ironic in a scientific context, one represented best in the episodes of the spiders' battle (described scientifically but also with knightly imagery) and in Richard's likening of football to war (and to life) in its challenge which can bring defeat.

Stallings is not just concerned with a wounded Marine — nor with a wounded nation — but with man and the wounds seemingly inherent in his participation in life. The predominant symbol of the work is the wound, and there are many. Man's wound is represented in each of seven generations of Plumes. Their names allegorically link them with Christian and historical tradition — Christian; Noah, Sr. and Jr.; George Washington; Zachary Taylor; Old Hickory; and Richard Coeur de Lion. Furthermore, such characters as Gary, the scientist, and Meyer, the conscientious objector and publisher, are also wounded. The nation's wound is represented by its crippled President, Woodrow Wilson. But there are also psychological wounds for all those in Woodland or in Washington who are struggling to reconcile war and romance, war and religion, or war and life. And Richard must cope with his desire for revenge.

The predominant imagery is that of Medieval Romance, which is represented best in the titles of the five books but also in the seasons, rituals (exchange of flowers), and courtly behavior of the characters. In sharp contrast is the scientific imagery inherent in numerous descriptions involving motion — waves and concentric circles. The impersonality of war and life is represented in kilowatt hours as Plume calculates the amount of sleep lost through pain:

First year . . . no sleep, hardly . . . say . . . two hours per night . . . normal sleep eight hours . . . loss of six hours. . . . Six hours times three sixty five nights in year equals . . . two thousand hundred and ninety hours. It pleased him to fancy some unit of measurement for pain; some method by which one might accurately measure the kilowatt hours of flow in each waking hour. Would be considered as force . . . electricity . . . volts, ohms, amperes . . . alternating by day, direct by night . . . be interesting to figure on ten million men wounded in last war . . . to total their kilowatt hours of pain.[70]

It is obvious here that the "ten million men" represent many wars and many periods of man. And Stallings is concerned about all their human suffering. At the time in human agony himself, Stallings considers the history of man, dating back to the "savages" who used "totem poles and scalps and piles of skulls."[71]

Beauty and happiness are associated only with myth (Daphne or a "Rodin mold"), and myth is associated with romance, especially for Esme who survives through her belief in myth. Perhaps Richard's reaction — and that of Stallings — is ironically a result of anguish at the loss of the myth (romance); and Stallings, through his predominant choice of romance imagery, suggests his own desire to recapture that elusive world as he begins, fictionally, to build his own mythical world.

III   Plumes *and* Sartoris

Plumes may have been a direct source for William Faulkner's later novel, *Sartoris* (1929), the first of his Yoknapatawpha saga, for there are too many similarities between the novels for them to be coincidental. (Stallings' story "Gentleman in Blue" and Faulkner's "Ambuscade" are equally similar.) Where Stallings traced the outmoded Romantic tradition through seven generations, Faulkner used three; and, just as each novel begins with the return of its World War I veteran, each ends with a cemetery scene. The swashbuckling, romantic ancestors of Richard Plume died absurd deaths just as old Colonel Sartoris died as a result of chasing after anchovies. Richard's father thought of himself as a "Bayard of a Southern Town"; and, in *Sartoris*, "Bayard" is the chief protagonist. But Plume's ancestors were more directly influenced by those knights of the Middle Ages, particularly through Froissart who provided Zachary Plume with his son's name, Richard Coeur de Lion. Old Colonel Sartoris read all "of Dumas," but his son Bayard "looked like Richard the First before he went crusading."

The two novels are similarly structured — five books in each. And, just as old Colonel Sartoris looms in the background throughout the five books of Faulkner's novel, Old Hickory Plume is ever-present through allusions to, or stories about, that gallant. Even the styles of the two novels are comparable. We may recall Stallings' calculation of the amount of sleep Plume lost through pain as Stallings considered the history of man dating back to the "savages" who used totem poles. A similar calculation occurs in *Sartoris* at the point where Aunt Jenny describes everyone as "savages"; Bayard thinks: "Three score and ten years to drag a stubborn body about the world and cozen its insistent demands. Three score and ten, the Bible said. Seventy years. And he was only twenty-six."

That Faulkner drew on Stallings, already famous in the 1920's, does not seem unlikely. (He knew Stallings and stayed with him in Hollywood for a short time.) Professor H. Edward Richardson, author of *William Faulkner: The Journey to Self-Discovery* (1969), agrees with my speculation and has discussed this with me.

IV *Autobiography, Guilt*

Stallings' novel includes more truth than fiction. It is, therefore, perhaps easier to cite some of the exceptions: unlike Richard and Esme, the Stallings had no children at that time. They had married after Stallings returned from war — not before he went. Like Plume, Stallings was offered an instructorship at Wake Forest; but, unlike Plume, he rejected it; instead, he accepted a position with the New York *World*. Stallings' first amputation occurred after a fall on ice rather than because of a physical attack on veterans. Furthermore, Stallings worked for the Washington *Times*, not the government nor a magazine. Plume's father had attended the same college and taught history as a profession; Stallings' father did not attend Wake Forest; and, while he taught Stallings quite a bit of history, teaching was not his profession.

We are especially aware of the theme of guilt reflected at a time when Stallings, the wounded veteran, tried to adjust to both civilian and married life. In *Plumes,* he had written of his inability to walk well: " . . . no man wishes to falter before the eyes of the woman he loves."[72] Since his earlier college days, young Plume "had always been afraid of her [Esme's] ridicule."[73] Life for his wife with a cripple added to Plume's guilt as he sought self-punishment from both friends and family. He wanted Dean Baylor to tell him that he "had made a hell of a mess"[74] of his life; in real life, Stallings felt much the same way.

While most of the novel is true, the changes serve, artistically, to allow Stallings' continuing dramatization of *leitmotifs* throughout history that he presents in the novel to emphasize his crusade against misguided romanticism. Writing as he searched in real life for its why's and absurdities, Stallings, at this point, respects no codes; for codes are inevitably linked with tradition. These, Stallings denies.

CHAPTER 3

Earth and Agape: The Plays

I What Price Glory?

A SPIRIT of camaraderie is more notable in *What Price Glory?* (co-authored with Maxwell Anderson) than the bitterness and disillusionment we might expect of the author of *Plumes.* The seriousness is present in Act II which, according to my best available sources, was written almost entirely by Stallings. Anderson had produced the basic plot with which he himself was dissatisfied. Stallings, then, apparently gave it life by rewriting and reworking the dialogue throughout the play.[1]

Produced in 1924, *What Price Glory?* became " . . . the most sensationally successful play of the . . . season."[2] Opening-night audiences were prepared for Realism by a "Note" in the program warning them that *What Price Glory?* was "a play of war as it is, not as it has been presented theatrically for thousands of years."[3] Although the language of the play seems much less bold today than that of almost any currently in production, to 1924 audiences the play was new — its action was made real, raw, by the dialogue.

The primary purpose of the play remained for Stallings simply the telling of the truth about war. But where *Plumes* was primarily a psychological response to the destruction of his illusions about war, *What Price Glory?* was a return from an esthetic distance to the war itself where these illusions were destroyed. And what was left man? Only earth, the natural appetites to be fulfilled, and *agape*, all made meaningful through competitive codes of conduct if man has a sense of humor, the ability to laugh at his own absurdity. Just as Stallings had represented the absurdity of life and war through irreconcilable oppositions in *Plumes,* he presented in the tragi-comic play these same absurdities, represented by such devices as games and obvious allegorical names for the characters.

Though Flagg is the major character in that action centers around him most of the time, there is no predominant hero in *What Price*

Glory? Each character represents a distinct characteristic of man responding to a particularly absurd situation. Together, they play the necessary games as they struggle to survive.[4] Almost forty years later Stallings referred to the *What Price Glory?* characters with the same expression used by Richard's father, Zachary, when he summed up the chronicler Froissart and named his son: "Whatever may have been their faults, there was not a coward among them."[5]

Stallings' presentation of attitudes in *What Price Glory?* seems to suggest that he is moving out of pure disillusionment toward a more objective viewpoint. Violence and nonviolence are present in action and in dialogue, but so is that buffoonery which so often accompanies any group of men in a situation demanding relief from the deadly game of war and its inescapable burden of fear.

What Price Glory? opens at Marine headquarters in a French farmhouse in 1918 where Marines Gowdy and Kiper are discussing Captain Flagg's monopoly of Cognac Pete's "available" daughter, Charmaine; the captain's anticipated trip to Paris; and the arrival of a new top soldier, Quirt. Captain Flagg respects Quirt's abilities as a sergeant; however, he leaves instructions for Charmaine to stay at home while he is away, since former experience has taught him not to trust Quirt with his women. Flagg leaves additional instructions for the Marines to keep an eye on Quirt because "Quirt loves the bottle; and when he's drunk he's the lousiest, filthiest bum that ever wore a uniform."[6] But it is Flagg who, on the way to Paris, gets drunk, is arrested, and never reaches the city. As soon as Flagg has left, Quirt begins flirting with Charmaine, who does not discourage his attention. Eight days later Flagg returns, discovers Charmaine's deception, and decides he will yet outdo Quirt. When Cognac Pete arrives and complains that daughter Charmaine's morals are ruined, Flagg tries to force Quirt to marry Charmaine. Quirt agrees until he discovers Flagg's intention to pull the company out shortly after the marriage ceremony, which never takes place.

When Act II opens in a cellar of a farmhouse near the battleground, Marine Aldridge has been wounded. Nearby, other Marines discuss the war until a young recruit, Moore, sees Aldridge's wounds and becomes hysterical. Flagg arrives to doctor Aldridge and to offer comfort to Moore while Quirt goes out to look around. When he returns with a slight wound in his leg, Flagg is certain that Quirt had deliberately "stuck out" his leg.[7] Quirt is ready to celebrate leaving the battle area and jokes about beating Flagg back to Charmaine. Suddenly a commotion above is heard, and three bombs explode. Flagg captures a German and is ready to dash off after Quirt when a young Marine, Lewisohn, is brought in wounded and cries for Flagg to stop his bleeding. Act II ends with Flagg's reassuring, "You'll be all right boy. You'll be all right. You'll be all right."[8]

Act III is set at Cognac Pete's tavern where Quirt arrives to spend a few minutes alone with Charmaine before Flagg returns. Flagg and Quirt get drunk enough to threaten each other as they play blackjack for a gun placed in the middle of the table. Quirt throws over the table, runs out into the dark, and leaves Flagg alone with Charmaine. When a "runner" arrives to announce that they are all leaving again, Quirt, by now hidden upstairs, overhears the orders and runs to join Flagg as the third act ends.

The competition for a dame is all a game, and is one no less absurd than the game of war. Charmaine may, allegorically, stand for France, the lady for whom they are all fighting; and, appropriately, no one but Charmaine seems to win. Indeed, games constitute the main action of the play. In addition to the game of love which Flagg and Quirt play with Charmaine, Cognac Pete plays his money game with Flagg; and Charmaine has several games going: romance with Flagg, romance with Quirt, and financial pawn for papa. All these games are set against the serious game of war. The only literal game — the card game — takes place near the end and brings the play to a climax. Ironically, neither Flagg nor Quirt permanently wins Charmaine — nor does either really want her when the bugle calls to war.

In Act II, the part of the play Stallings wrote almost entirely, some of the same attacks voiced by Richard Plume are echoed in the younger Marines' conversation about war. Marine Kiper feels no shame in saying, "I don't want no more."[9] Another — Lipinsky — is sure he will live through it; but, when Kiper asks, "How do you know . . . Said your prayers, I suppose, and got an answer," Lipinsky wants no answer "from that bird. . . . He'd send the answer collect, and it would say, 'Fall in and get the manure outta the French angels' backyards. Clean up heaven, you low-down Marine, so's the National Guard won't get typhoid when they all die and come here.' "[10]

Kiper can declare that there "ain't any heaven" only to be told by the Mate, "You birds know your souls go somewheres. You've seen too many men die." But Kiper feels that he has more important things to worry about: "That soul ain't any of my business. It ain't got to eat; it ain't got to run; it ain't got to stand in line ten days a

week to sign the payroll. I should get on my ear about where this
doodlebug in my chest is going after I die. It ain't never helped me
none. It can go to hell for all I care."[11] This scene is reminiscent of
one in *Plumes* where Richard refers to his Christian background,
which is as little comfort to him when he is suffering as it is to Kiper,
who, like Plume, would think such things only "cruel
superstitions."[12] A concern with survival on earth, here and now,
dominates in the play as it had in *Plumes*.

In this same scene, the young Marine, Moore, in the lengthiest
speech of the play, lashes out at the whole miserable mess of war:

> God DAMN them for keeping us up in this hellish town. Why can't they
> send in some of the million men they've got back there and give us a
> chance? Men in my platoon are so hysterical every time I get a message from
> Flagg, they want to know if they're being relieved. What can I tell them?
> They look like whipped dogs — as if I had just beaten them — and I've had
> enough of them this time. I've got to get them out, I tell you. They've had it.
> Every night the same way. And since six o'clock there's been a wounded
> sniper in the trees by that orchard angle crying "Kamerad!" Just like a big
> crippled whippoorwill. What price glory now? Why in God's name can't we
> all go home? Who gives a damn for this lousy, stinking little town but the
> poor French bastards who live here? God damn it! You talk about courage,
> and all night long you hear a man who's bleeding on a tree calling you
> "Kamerad" and asking you to save him. God damn every son of a bitch in
> the world who isn't here! I won't stand for it! I won't stand for it! I won't
> have the platoon asking me every minute of the livelong night when they are
> going to be relieved. . . . Flagg, I tell you you can shoot me, but I won't
> stand for it. . . . I'll take 'em out tonight and kill you if you get in my way.[13]

This passage expresses an attitude towards war that is quite similar to
Richard Plume's brief but objective statement that the experience
was the same for men on both sides — a remark made when he
recalls killing the German boy who had been fed propaganda similar
to that he had heard. Also, Moore's damning all those who are not
there corresponds to Richard's recollection of his wound: "The God-
damned scoundrelly orators were not there. . . ."[14]

Comforting Moore in fatherly tones, Flagg responds to the dis-
traught Marine with *"a gentility never before* revealed."[15] Flagg's
effort distinguishes him from the younger Quirt; otherwise, little distinction exists, other than rank and age, between the two main
characters. The older Marines are all perhaps a little braver or can
put up a better front. (Richard Plume had heard "something

whisper" that " . . . a bold front is half the battle.") Ferguson, a regular, is used to being left behind: "Twenty years now I've had 'em leave me. When I was younger I believed some of the liars who said they liked to fight . . . liked being under fire. . . ."[16] But no one in *What Price Glory?* thinks or says that he likes to fight. Flagg pretends to be tougher than he is. He can be gentle when he has to play father, but he raves when off duty about wanting no part of "green troops." Quirt is a younger Flagg, experienced and capable; but he is not there for fun.

Charmaine is the only female character in the play. She likes handsomely decorated American males, and they all like her. Flagg and Quirt are only two of the many admirers she has known. Her father, "Cognac Pete," is more colorful; as guardian of Charmaine's virtue (in cash-register terms), he knows how to manipulate Flagg. By threatening a suit, he sends Flagg running for papers immediately, and Flagg makes financial arrangements to satisfy Pete. The role of one other character, the General, is not unimportant, though minor. He comes to Flagg's office with all the seriousness of the high command, bringing orders for Flagg to "get through the German lines some night and tack up posters" which have been sent over by "some Yankee Doodle back in Hoboken. . . ."[17] He also instructs Flagg to bring back a German prisoner. The brief scene between the two burlesques the fantastic concepts of war of the people back home; and the General is a caricature of a tottering old fool who understands little about the real front. Quick, witty, subtle, the remarks against those who lack comprehension of war are never out of place; but they are not so bold as the open criticism of war, politicians, and military commanders since the 1960's.

Comedy in Act I becomes tragedy in Act II; but a return to comedy occurs in Act III. The transition is made smoothly because of Stallings' dialogue in Act II. Seriousness is confined mainly to the minor characters, while jesting between Quirt and Flagg continues throughout the play. Both thoroughly masculine, they seem to thrive on competition; and, although they are not unaware of the suffering around them, they never talk about it. Their conversation is primarily limited throughout all three acts to the topic of Charmaine. And their competition, in love and war, includes only one code of conduct: anything goes, but the best man will win.

In many ways *What Price Glory?* differs from *Plumes* and its emphasis on suffering and disillusionment. A postwar reaction, *Plumes* was released only months before the production of *What*

Price Glory? Yet, in the play, the tone and the total attitude toward war represent a more balanced portrayal of opposites: frivolity and competition are juxtaposed with serious disparagement and death; love games and war games; inexperienced and experienced soldiers. And there are the young and innocent along with the mature and not-so-innocent. All the characters, moreover, are not wounded as most were in *Plumes.* But everyone and everything has its price — participation in any experience at a given time or age probably determines what price glory? Charmaine's moment of glory is the most trivial; to her, glory may be having many available American males. Moore's moment of martial glory is marred by a painful wound that affects his reaction erratically. For old Ferguson, glory may lie in watching the survivors return from battle; and, for Quirt, glory is usually no more than out-fighting or out-loving Flagg and getting away from the grimy battlefield as fast as possible. For Flagg, it may seem to the viewer that his glory is in being a top soldier, in staying alive, and in training others so that they may survive. But, for all of them, "glory" is a term used back home for all those who have experienced fighting for "Old Glory." None is concerned with glory in the sense that a man may traditionally achieve it in battle.[18]

The use of "price," however, suggests that, despite the fact that experience costs something, whether it be the loss of innocence or life, it is difficult to determine price in terms of military glory since glory is itself a relative term. Perhaps there was no glory at all associated with a war that was, in a sense, a dress rehearsal for a later, bigger war. Like the action of the play, the interlude between battles barely provides time for recuperation. The call to arms is unpredictable, but there is always the next call. And, despite fatigue or lack of training, the men go to battle. Much of this perpetual response to war is revealed in Stallings' later stories about the "real doughboys." War is not glorious, but man is — especially the man, who, tested by fire, retains a balance in life, a love for his fellow man, and a sense of humor — represented appropriately in the play through the final action of Quirt who runs to join Flagg with "Hey Flagg, wait for baby!" — the closing line of the play.

An understanding of Stallings as a man and a writer would lead any student of his work to suspect that there is much more in the play than soldiers' using rough language and men's making war seem like fun, as some critics considered the play. Described as cynical by other critics, *What Price Glory?* evoked numerous responses and was the subject of much conversation at the time of its production. Burns Mantle, editor of *The Best Plays of 1924-25*, wrote in the introduction to the play: " . . . debaters on either side of an argument to sustain or disprove the [Heywood] Broun contention that *What Price Glory?* is, in fact, the oft-quoted great American play will at least know they have been in a fight. Which, of itself, proves that it is a great play."[19] Mantle's own attitude toward *What Price Glory?* was expressed in his opening paragraph:

The Pulitzer prize was given to another play, but in the estimation of most of those who take their drama seriously in this theatrical captital *What Price Glory?* held a comfortable lead as the most significant drama of the year, as it was, unquestionably, the outstanding success of the season. . . . It represents war . . . as it is in truth and in fact, and there is pretty general agreement with the estimate of Heywood Broun who wrote that "This is certainly the best use which the theatre has yet made of the war, and it is entirely possible that it is the best American play about anything."

While most critics praised the play in general terms, Joseph Wood Krutch, with whom I agree, presented one of the few close readings of the play:

. . . the purpose of the play was to discover how the experience of two uncultivated but emancipated individuals who found themselves commited to a conflict which they were unable to idealize could be arranged into a satisfactory pattern. In another age their experiences would have taken shape around ideas of patriotism, heroism, and honor. Their exhaltations and their sufferings would have acquired a meaning by reference to these fixed points. But for these particular heroes these particular fixed points no longer existed. They could no more reconcile themselves to their adventures by conceiving themselves as heroic defenders of a mystic fatherland than they could dignify their interlude with the farmer's buxom daughter by attributing to it the traditional values of romantic love. When life becomes as painful and as precarious as theirs was, then the human need to make life justify itself becomes desperately acute, and, in their case, the justification had to be made in terms of that witty animality which alone had been left them.[20]

However, Krutch's summing up of the character Flagg may be exaggerated: He describes him as excessively brutal, as cultivating "drunkenness and lust . . . not because of any innate depravity, but because they alone are anodynes powerful enough . . . to drug such an existence." In his eagerness to make Flagg represent dehumanized war, Krutch may overstate Flagg's brutality; for the tender scenes between Flagg and Moore or Flagg and Lewisohn reveal that Flagg can be a warm, understanding, and compassionate man, who, despite the mess of things, gives encouragement and solace to his men.

One other criticism is worth noting. Arthur Hobson Quinn, in "The New Realism of Character," wrote that " . . . the philosophy of war from the point of view of a sergeant was explained with a profanity which was perhaps unnecessarily violent for the purpose of art. Some of the play, like the episode of the General and his staff, was absurd, but the scene in the dugout cellar in a disputed town was masterly."[21] What Quinn fails to understand was that the absurdity was intentional and was more significant in a play treating some of the absurdities of war and life. Moreover, Quinn misjudges the characters Flagg and Quirt: "They hate each other, for past rivalries and injuries, and their rivalry is made concrete by their passing passion for Charmaine. . . . " Part of the significance of such a scene in which Quirt and Flagg wrestle for a gun is that it reflects the immediate brutalizing effect on man of war which dehumanizes what might be the closest friendship. But their quarrel is forgotten as soon as the call to arms comes, and the two who dash to battle again are not the two men who hate each other. Even Quinn notes that the end — "the quiet immediate response to duty, without display" — lifts *What Price Glory?* "out of melodrama into something higher."

Even though *What Price Glory?* evoked many different responses as well as different degrees of enthusiasm, the important fact about the play was its acceptable but strong attack on war in a tragi-comic manner.[22] It staged for the first time, as realistically as possible, an event that had changed the lives of millions everywhere; and it expressed an outlook on war shared by many at the time. Harlan Hatcher, under the heading "The War Generation," summarized the play's significance in one statement: "*What Price Glory?* did more than any single novel on the same theme to define the point of view of the twenties."[23]

Though it is almost impossible to determine specific autobiographical relations represented in *What Price Glory?*, there are clearly some real sources and influences. Stallings again drew on his own wartime experience in writing the dialogue, a fact already mentioned in my treatment of the similarities between action and dialogue in the play and in *Plumes*. But Stallings, well known by his contemporaries for his sense of humor, allows humor to permeate more of the play than it had of the novel. In the novel, humor was confined primarily to his description of earlier ancestors; and even then the tone was often sardonic. Little or no humor could be found in the lives of Esme and Richard Plume. Increasingly, Stallings seems, therefore, to have tempered his own disillusionment with humor as he moved toward a more objective attitude toward war and life in *What Price Glory?*

II First Flight *and* The Buccaneer

Stallings collaborated with Maxwell Anderson on two other plays, *First Flight* and *The Buccaneer*, which were both produced in 1925. Neither, however, was so successful on the stage as *What Price Glory?*[24] Neither is related to war, but both include historical heroes, who are significant only in their own historical context. After all, Stallings had been reared with such heroes as Robert E. Lee, Stonewall Jackson, and Andrew Jackson verbally present; and his disillusionment, as presented in *Plumes*, stemmed from the destruction of ideals associated with romanticized versions of history — especially the Civil War. Then too, Stallings was suffering from the physical and psychological pain of the loss of a leg, a loss which seems to have made it necessary that he prove continually his manhood. So it seems natural that he turn to the rougher, tougher, more virile and roguish type of hero of the past as he struggles to regain the identity lost with the destruction of his illusions, his heroes, and his leg. Captain Flagg had these roguish and rough characteristics. Now, Stallings portrays similar qualities in historical heroes while, at the same time, reflecting the effect of his own loss. To borrow his own phraseology, we may regard him at this time as "building temples"[25] to his gods, ones which he hopes look like him.

First Flight is a portrait of young Andrew Jackson, a lawyer representing the State of North Carolina and sent to Nashville to deal with Tennesseans who prefer forming a separate state. Young Jackson's "first flight" is from romance, an obvious deterrent to his political career, yet a basic and necessary experience in his maturation. Juxtaposing the admirable qualities, both physical and mental, of a leader with the genteel, romantic characteristics of the man, Stallings portrays a man in whom the common man of the nineteenth century later found expression. Appealing to both male and female by his mixture of virility and leadership, Jackson outwits the suitors of the lovely Miss Charity,[26] who is affected by what she considers the charm of Jackson's innocence and his starts toward success. Action continues to be a game motif: the game of love and the game of politics are both revealed during a card game. Winning at cards, love, and politics, Jackson can leave Charity, who, like Charmaine, takes chances with several available men.

Another game of love and adventure, *The Buccaneer* is set in the 1600's in Panama City when it was captured by the pirate and adventurer, Sir Henry Morgan. The play includes numerous love escapades as Morgan goes from woman to woman, but the action concentrates on one in particular, Lady Neville. She understands Morgan's game of courtly love and reads to him from Chaucer's *Troilus*. Without meaning to, she falls for the adventurous rogue. Captured and returned to England for trial, Morgan advises Charles II who is not quite sure that he can completely excuse Morgan's crimes. The king does, however, and Morgan prepares at the end of the play to leave for ore adventure. Morgan's final, rather long speech as he prepares to leave is important to this study:

Am I a game cock, to put on exhibition? I'll tell you what I think of this town and of you all. You're a scrambling of all the petty thieves and faint hearts that don't dare go out and loot for yourselves, a heap of leaners and hangers-on, afraid to go your own way, dragging on each other for support and licking the king's boots for him, so he'll let you live. And look at your courtiers — how long would they last on the deck of a man-o-war? The deck of a man-o-war's the place for a man. There's beauty and courage and fighting blood on the deck of a ship of the line. . . . I'm off for Jamaica, gentlemen and ladies, and God forgive you for a parcel of nincompoops. Unless, by chance, I'm mistaken, and there's a man among you — just one. On that chance, gentlemen, a last call for volunteers. . . . Who'll follow Sir Henry Morgan to the Caribbean and the Spanish Main? Who's sick of living at the rotten center of an empire?

Lady Neville picks up the glove Morgan has tossed on the floor and joins him as the play ends.

The style of the passage is unmistakably Stallings' and suggests something of the fascination with adventure which he associates with a "man-o-war." Written by a man whose masculinity and virility were often defined in his pursuit of daredevil adventure, Stallings reveals in this passage something of the effect on him of the loss of his leg: "Am I a game cock to put on exhibition?" Memories of what he can momentarily recall as "beauty and courage and fighting blood on the deck of a ship" are important in his readjustment to society as a crippled man. And the recollection is unmistakably romantic as Stallings concentrates on courage. In the plays, death is still important: several killings occur in *The Buccaneer*, though Morgan actually kills no one, but young Jackson in *First Flight* kills a man who drunkenly assaults him before a scheduled duel is to take place. And Jackson and Morgan show little fear in their confrontation with death. Both *First Flight* and *The Buccaneer* put literal romance second to the romance of adventure, and the main characters of each play represent the appeal of the highly individualistic, masculine character who is especially self-assured.

There may be biographical irony in Morgan's reference to the "leaners" and "hangers-on."[27] For a man like Stallings, adjusting to the loss of a limb was extremely difficult; yet those who knew him have observed that he always made light of it. His devotion to the very masculine hero may have been therapeutic, and it may relate to his own later search for adventure. Significantly, the more fiction he wrote, the greater became his concern for adventure; and he wrote less about the relationship between men and women, particularly in the short stories.[28]

CHAPTER 4

Vale of Tears: The Short Stories

ALL but one of Stallings' published war stories are set in the context of World War I, and these stories constitute brief vignettes which serve to complete the story of Richard Plume's wartime experience. In the novel *Plumes*, action and time shift from the opening portrait of the physically healthy young Marine to his return, severely wounded, to this country from France. Except for the one stream-of-consciousness recollection of Richard's wound, no descriptions of battles or of the long hospital experience in France are included. The space between Plume, would-be warrior, and Plume wounded, is devoted to the flashback presentation of the Plume ancestry; and in the time between these two looks at Plume, Stallings returns for short-story material.

I "The Big Parade"

During Plume's lowest moment, as he is rushed to the Washington hospital, he recalled "Parades and parades and parades."[1] Earlier he had asked Gary, "Ever hear the first sharp note of adjutant's call, on the morning of a big parade?"[2] As Stallings recalls the irony of his early attraction to such pomp and show, he presents an opposite viewpoint of "the big parade" in his story by that title (1924). "The Big Parade" includes only one named character — Gianonni, a "dark, unleashed undertaker's assistant from Brooklyn."[3] One of "nine surviving men," he is under the command of an unnamed lieutenant who is the central intelligence of the story.

Gianonni is described as a man who "was wonderful about the dead; [he] put them out of sight before morning, threw a light mantle of earth over their drained faces, replenished mantles of other nights where desecrating shells had churned the light, odorous loam of spring." He carries messages and is, as the lieutenant recalls, "the best runner in the world."

The Lieutenant had received a message from headquarters instructing him to bring eight men to battalion headquarters "to entrain for Paris." There, they would "represent the regiment in a Fourth of July parade."[4] The lieutenant concentrates briefly on the "sinister moral" of the expedition: "Dirtied Americans, smelling of blood, were to be exhibited along the Champs Elysees fresh from the lines. The French, become connoisseurs in enervated faces, could find proof of active American participation in the *seven kinds of hell* prepared for a sister republic."[5] He thinks about the ninety men of the original company, of whom only nine remain. He would like to take all nine, for all are anxious to get away from the battlefield. But, when they draw straws, Gianonni has to stay behind. During the parade, the lieutenant thinks of Gianonni and pretends that he is behind him. By the time the parade is over, he knows that Gianonni is dead.

To paraphrase "The Big Parade" does the author an injustice; for the story renders, vividly, an experience that in its range is sensuous, emotional, and imaginative. Stallings gives no long description of the actual parade; indeed, only one paragraph is devoted to the event, and then emphasis is upon the aching feet of men who would gladly continue to walk rather than return to war: "The twisting mass of weary men streamed through avenues of green, canyons of white stucco, hordes of clacking tongues. The lieutenant grew weary, faint, bored again. He would have continued walking through eternity had he been offered the alternative to the lines. . . . Men lifted aching feet from underneath other aching feet and cursed solid sheets of profanity. Sweat enriched the smells of them again, and the lieutenant cursed too. They were restoring his eight to him, and Gianonni was not among them."[6]

The men are not cowards, but they hate war's destruction and feel the futility of life at the front. Their participation in a parade in support of war reflects men as weary of the times as in their bones, but they are willing to be displayed if doing so means leaving the front. None is interested in the parade which, having lost its glamour by now, serves ironically as a brief but tiring respite. The lieutenant's concern for the only missing member, Gianonni, is touching but not sentimental.

There is little extensive development of action or of character in so short a story (originally five typed sheets), but the main emphasis is upon the irony or the absurdity of the experience. A soldier may be fascinated with the posters and the parades which contributed to his recruitment, but in this story the parade merely serves as relief from the battle zone. There is no concern for the adjutant's bugle call or for displaying one's adorned physique. Only the weariness — in the tone and in the constant concern with death hovering in the rear — impresses the reader. Irony is implicit in Giannonni's death because he drew the wrong straw in a "game." Much more subtle than either *Plumes* or *What Price Glory?*, the story lacks the passionate, disillusioning comments of the novel, and the camaraderie of the play. Moreover, all that we usually equate with parades is missing; in fact, the parade becomes, in a sense, a death march.[7]

II *"Esprit de Corps"*

The shift in Stallings' attitude from *Plumes* to that displayed in the second act of *What Price Glory?* is comparable to the difference between "The Big Parade" (1924) and his next story, "Esprit de Corps" (1928). This story is set in a Red Cross tent where several wounded men wait quietly, it seems, for death.[8] The cross on the top of the tent is described by Stallings as one which "stands for humanity as defined by the Geneva convention," but it also serves "as a marker for airplanes." A Marine major and several of his men in the tent had been wounded when "an airplane returning from Paris with a leftover bomb" dropped "it into the hospital yard for a lark."[9] The major, unnamed, who had "kept to himself in his life" and was "reserved in his death" prefers "dying impersonally."[10] Dying of a gangrenous shoulder, he lies "observing the progress of enemy troops against the citadel of his heart." His adjutant dies quietly, and the orderlies place his body "on the litter and lurch across the grass.[11] As the dead body is carried away, the major salutes "vacantly": "The mechanical excellence of the salute dispelled any gathering emotionalism in the tent. Only an old fellow, a marine gunner, sat upright and peered at the pall."[11]

All is silent until a Naval doctor arrives, and the major hears him comment that "the infantry starts at four, and we'll have some of them at six."[12] The doctor reminds the men that "the army brigade . . . has been itching for the chance" to fight because "the marines have been featured in all the dispatches." One quiet "giant" rears up to respond to the doctor: "Those doughboys'll just naturally kill themselves some Heinies this morning, sir. They want to be in the newspapers, just like the marines."[13] Such is the spirit of the corps as the major continues to survey "the battle around the citadel of his heart."[14] Finally, an army captain is brought in wounded, and the silence of the tent suddenly becomes a shouting exchange between him and the Marine major. The story closes with a nurse's shushing them.

"Esprit de Corps" moves rapidly from a serious, somber opening to a wild exchange of yelling and cursing at the end. As each man boasts proudly of his own outfit, each reveals his pride, a pride very much alive whenever his outfit's accomplishments are challenged.[15] Even the Marine major, who cannot live, momentarily forgets the gangrenous shoulder. War is no less cruel, but the men who fight it and are wounded talk less about its cruelties — and such is also the case with Stallings. The competitive spirit of Captain Flagg and Sergeant Quirt is magnified and telescoped in the story to show that the competitive spirit may help men die proudly. There is no disillusionment in "Esprit de Corps," and the story stands in sharp contrast to *Plumes*. But the reality of the story is a wounded reality in which men, accustomed to death, bravely cope with its existence.

By the time Stallings published this story (1928), he had adjusted to a wooden leg; but what has been described as his "stump" nearly drove him to insanity because it refused to "knit."[16] The success of his novel *Plumes*, the play *What Price Glory?*, and the stipends from the movies *The Big Parade* and *What Price Glory?* had made him financially independent. He had, in a few short years, accomplished much and had met many new, exciting, and competitive people while working for the New York *World* (1922-1926). In short, he had recaptured his ability to face and to enjoy life's challenges. His future looked bright, and the horrors of the battlefield had somewhat diminished though he would always walk on the grim World-War-I souvenir. His adjustment should not be overly simplified; but his strong determination to cope with his existence was, perhaps, though ironically so, linked to his successes as a writer.

In his novel, Plume had said, "I am all cerebral from now on. No walks, no trees, no fields, no sky. All books."[17] But he had also said that people should read economics and not sentimental pieces: "An economist does not have to go out and dig for specimens of gold."[18] Plume had failed physically in that he would never be whole again. His creator, Stallings, felt that it was especially important to succeed intellectually because he too had been wounded. And New York provided ample competition in a world where few, if any, had equaled his accomplishments with a first novel, play, short story, and movie. What other American writer could claim such successful versatility, particularly in regard to one subject? Certainly his achievement must have seemed equal to his earlier successes, determined by physical prowess and fortitude, whether as a football player in college or a war hero in France. Thus, the shift in attitude occurs, and Stallings' next published story, "Turn Out the Guard" (1928) reflects a much happier man whose recollection of his war experience is opposite to that of Plume.

III   *"Turn Out The Guard"*

"Turn Out the Guard" is sometimes a funny story, for no fighting, no wounding, no war horror occurs — on the surface or in the background. Divided into four parts, the story opens in April, 1917, with Colonel Stonewall Jackson Butt, a West Pointer, "cooling his heels in the Canal Zone"[19] while awaiting the arrival of his son, an officer in the navy and a graduate of Annapolis. As Part II opens, the father is "Brigadier General Butt"; the son, "Lieutenant — senior grade"[20]; and in Parts III and IV, they are, respectively, "Major General Butt" and "Lieutenant Commander Butt, Jr." The promotion in rank is due to the marriage of young Butt to the daughter of a "member of the House Committee on Naval Affairs."[21]

Part I includes the serious attitudes of the Butts, Army and Navy, who hold the prejudices of separate branches of the service. Young Butt makes excuses for his father's absence from the front: " 'My father,' he said, 'is a Bayardist — a fellow who believes in leading his troops. If he were sent to France, his bloody pugnacity would result in his being made a major general. But regardless of rank he would *lead the first wave* of any operation he might be supposed to direct. This would result in his death. But the War Department believes that the only bad major general is a dead major general. Obviously, it will keep him at Panama for the duration.' "[22] Colonel Butt has other plans, and not long after his son's arrival he has introduced his son to his future wife, Wanda, daughter of Porcinus, a congressman.

In Part II, the son has married; and both men are on their way to France. When the father meets his son, he has to admit that he is to be "acclimatized in the Service of Supply. 'Potatoes,' he said, with some bitterness." His son promises a change; and in Part III, his father is an inspector. The son is "in potatoes." When his wife, Wanda, and his father-in-law, Porcinus, visit his kitchen, young Butt, annoyed by their meddling, orders them out. The shocked congressman shouts angrily, "I'll have you recalled from France. I'll order an investigation of your career." But his son-in-law leaves with the remark "investigate and be damned."[23]

In Part IV, his father arrives for inspection, and a Marine sergeant who had been watching "for his passage since sunrise bawls, 'Turn Out the Guard.' " The same sergeant later gives an absurd explanation for a missing button, and he is rewarded for his ingenuity by Brigadier General Butt, who announces that the sergeant is his "first choice" to be sent "to the noncommissioned officers' school at Gondrecourt."[24] The general pronounces "a perfect inspection" despite rusty rifles, missing buttons, and tattoos showing; and the officers go in to lunch to toast the "Democratic Party . . . that is making the world safe for Democracy."[25]

Obviously satiric, the story is often concerned with absurdities which, presented humorously, are related to trivia. Criticism is not limited to any one branch of the service but to ranking officers in general and to academy-produced officers in particular. Stallings includes little character description; the characters, as if in a stage production, are revealed through conversation and incidents. The entire story is an expansion of a similarly brief idea from *What Price Glory?* — specifically, that of the general who gave Flagg instructions to cross enemy lines to tack up posters.

But Stallings is actually recalling — and having fun doing so — some of the many characters he knew during World War I, characters he later portrayed in *The Doughboys* (1963).[26] The germ of this story may be found in *Plumes*. Richard has his first glimpse of his fourth cousin Jabez, an army veteran and a congressman, talking to his son who is in the navy: " 'What a come down!' his thoughts danced. 'A Plume in the navy.' "[27]

The buffoonery which is juxtaposed with seriousness in *What Price Glory?* is enlarged to exclude any seriousness as Stallings takes jabs at the Democratic party, which is symbolically represented as a petticoat power since Wanda, daughter of the congressman, controls the future of the males represented. Moreover, as we have already observed, Stallings makes no biting comments and includes no sad scenes. The only reference to any wound appears at the very end when Lieutenant Butt, Jr., decides that he is "beginning to love Wanda, just as Wanda was probably preparing to send him to sea. Easiest way to make it up would be to get a wound. Wounds, though, were scarce as hen's teeth in howitzers. He knew Wanda, though. She'd never rest until she had christened his own battleship."[28]

The implication is that the courtly male will do anything for his lady's love or attention — even to the point of dying — and that the female is selfishly predatory. And, while Stallings jests, the implication is not so distantly removed from the glory-seeking football player, Richard Plume, who had hoped that Esme would "admire him for having something in him which made him helpless before the call of football."[29] Though the tone indeed contrasts, Stallings is again criticizing tradition in "the system" as he moves toward a more objective view of earlier experiences.

IV "Vale of Tears"

Stallings returns in his next story, "Vale of Tears," first published in *Cosmopolitan* in 1931, to the spirit of "Esprit de Corps," his longest story, which is more nearly a novella. Set in a hospital ward "at Angers," the story spans the last three months of 1918 and ends on Christmas Eve. Though the Armistice occurred on November 11, it is only casually alluded to among wounded men who are more concerned with coping with the monotony of each day.

As the story opens, Hugh Dozier, age twenty, has been hospitalized for four months without seeing anyone from his old outfit, "the 47th Company, 3rd Battalion, Second Division of the Marines. . . . He was lonely for men who had seen the things he had seen."[30] News arrives shortly that a "convoy of wounded from the Second Division" is expected, and Dozier places his Marine cap on the bed post so that it will be recognized by anyone from his outfit.

Nearby, Captain Jackson, tattooed with religious and patriotic pictures,[31] watches for someone who had been at Saint-Mihiel when he was wounded. He wants to know what happened. When the convoy finally arrives, one Marine, Terrence Delaney, though wearing a black patch over one eye, recognizes Dozier's cap, stops the orderlies, and inquires about Dozier. "For the first time in four months"[32] young Dozier feels fine. Delaney is taken to the dark room, and Dozier orders quail to be cooked, sends him wine and cigars, and welcomes his comrade in the grand style. Meantime, Dr. Cross informs Dozier of Delaney's real wound "in the worst place,"[33] and the men are immediately sympathetic. Captain Jackson declares that, if he were a fellow Marine, he would give Delaney a gun; but Dozier shrugs: "It's not everything in life." When they later discover that Delaney has a gun, Jackson comments, "It must be a powerfully comforting thing. It gives the imagination a jumping-off place, and saves the fancy from . . . wandering down the impossible halls of the future."[34]

After two weeks in the dark room, Delaney joins the others in the ward. "Travelling-salesman" jokes are suddenly taboo because the men do not want to remind Delaney of his wound. Conversation centers on battles of the Bible — discussed in war terminology. And, for those who prefer not to talk, "A.P.O.N." ("ain't putting out nothing") is the answer: "The letters were code for a gasping man who wished to be let very much alone."[35] While Jackson continues to keep the ward "barren of love lore," Dozier, who is in love with nurse Adair,[36] is persuaded by her to move to a vacant spot beside Delaney — to help him take an interest in life. A new patient — a preacher — arrives as another patient leaves, dead.

The first response from Delaney is roused by Jackson, who, trying to make the preacher talk, comments: "This would be a lot finer war if the churches instead of being for it, were dead set against it. Give it the irresistible appeal to the youth of the country, and dispense with recruiting posters."[37] Delaney discloses the fact that he was a divinity student. After hearing the preacher say, "I think the churches will lose caste by sponsoring the war," Delaney angrily shouts: "You are wrong about the churches. It's their ideal. The young man who is torn apart to save the race. It's their story. They can't welsh on their own story."[38] When asked what he would be, Delaney answers: "There's a divinity that shapes our ends, you know. . . ."[39] That night Delaney slips out; and Dozier, etherized from another operation, is wakened from a bad dream by the nurse, who is certain that Delaney will kill himself. After they have heard a "shout below, and a joyous bellow of 'Turn Out the Guard!' "[40] Delaney wanders in, drunk and singing.

Action shifts to Christmas Eve as the story closes. Dozier's cast is removed, and he and Jackson prepare to spend a lonely Christmas after Delaney borrows Dozier's money and leaves. Dr. Cross, married to nurse Adair that day, says goodbye to his patients as he gets ready to go to Germany. Dozier says goodbye with "big tears in his eyes"[41] as he and Jackson sip rum and wish for a chimney piece on which to hang their plaster casts.

Echoes of the disappointment expressed in *Plumes* are heard again in "Vale of Tears." While the story is, by Stallings' own account, a portrait of himself as Hugh Dozier,[42] it differs from his other fiction in the more restrained style in which it is presented. The only brief impassioned response is Delaney's — concerning the churches' role in war. But the relationship between Stallings' treatment of the church and war, or of God and man's suffering, is the same.

We are rarely conscious of an outside world when reading "Vale of

Tears." Only the nurses and the doctors come and go from the ward as wounded patients enter and as the dead are carried out. Acceptance of a situation which the men neither caused nor could change dominates the moods of most of them. We almost forget that death is serious among those who are very much alive despite their wounds. No one mentions courage, but it is everywhere present. Delaney's brief escape and the reference to the "bellow" heard are narrated but not treated in relationship to the outside world. But no one completely disintegrates, and everyone tries to help each other — except Delaney, who, ironically, commands the most respect. He is the only one who can get his way with the tough nurse, Miss Broadus.

Using a different spelling, Stallings once referred to this story as "Veil of Tears."[43] No longer openly expressing his grief, he may have considered it to be literally veiled in the story. "Vale" in Latin means "farewell," and the story is, in a sense, Stallings' farewell to any published, fictional recollection of his hospital experience, whether overseas or in this country where his legs were finally amputated.

The story could be described as the prelude to Hemingway's earlier work, *The Sun Also Rises*. As if Stallings had dwelt on the material that would have preceded that novel's beginning, he writes of a character very like Jake Barnes, for his wound was the same as Delaney's. But Stallings' story differs in tone and theme from Hemingway's novel: what could have been a disillusioning story of death or sterility is, instead, a story of men whose sense of humor and whose spirit of camaraderie allow them to cope with their isolated and wounded existence.

When Richard Plume met a fellow Marine from his old division, it "aroused no feeling of camaraderie."[44] But Stallings' characters, no longer self-centered, show concern for other wounded veterans. They respect each other — a respect implicit in their personal codes. Although compassion and love exist, the men evoke no pity; and the only tears are not from pain but because of separation of friends. There is *agape*.

By the time he wrote, "Vale of Tears," Stallings had, in 1930, adapted Hemingway's *A Farewell to Arms* for the stage. Stallings' use of the shorter, simpler sentence in "Vale of Tears" suggests the Hemingway influence. A sustained pace runs throughout the story. Perhaps Stallings is competing with Hemingway in style as well as in content by drawing on his own hospital experience, which was a reminder of his greater personal loss and of his authority to describe more accurately those grievous days of the really wounded. In short, he may have been trying to "out-truth" Hemingway.

V *"Gentleman in Blue"*

The more simple and direct style of "Vale of Tears" is continued in Stallings' next story, "Gentleman in Blue," which was selected for *The Best Short Stories of 1932;* this tale is Stallings' only published Civil War story though he wrote at least one other, "Yellow Tavern," his favorite.[45] In keeping with his determination not to romanticize the past, Stallings tells a simple story which is narrated retrospectively by an unnamed boy. He recalls in the first person the day a group of Yankee soldiers appeared at his home near the town of Amelia. Because his father and brothers were away fighting with the Confederates, he, his mother, and several Negro servants were alone. As the soldiers approach, Amos, the butler, brings Miss Sarah a rifle; and she walks out to meet the men in blue. In gentlemanly tones, one tall man asks for "fire to light" their pipes, and Miss Sarah instructs Amos to "take a shovel of fire down to the gentlemen . . ." for she is "sure that they are gentlemen"[46]; but Amos is not so certain. After thanking Miss Sarah, the men prepare to ride away; but she calls to them, offering to share her bread and butter; the men join her in the dining room. The boy is frightened but impressed by the glaring blue uniforms. His mother reassures him that their "very blue coats" are "their only difference from"[47] the Confederate soldiers. During their conversation at the table, the boy's mother learns that the war is almost over and that the men will soon be coming home:

> "It'll be over by tomorrow or next day," the Yankee was saying. "We're Sheridan's men. All of us are back of him, and he can't possibly get out."
> "Back of father?" I asked, frightened.
> "Back of General Lee," mother said. "My father's the best one of General Lee's men," I said.
> "He's a wonderful man then," the Yankee said. He had finished his bread. "We must go on," he said. "We might bring something down upon this house, remaining here." He got up from the table, and he bowed, and remained bowing until mother left the dining room holding my hand. "We are deeply grateful," she said.[48]

Later, the boy and his mother hear guns; and, after running to an upstairs window, they see Confederate soldiers following the

Yankees who try to re-enter her gate; but their leader, the tall man in blue, prevents it. However, the boy and his mother see the Yankee fall from his horse; and Miss Sarah and Amos rush out to bring him into the house. The story concludes quickly with a statement that the boy spent the next two days at his Uncle Billy's; and, when he returned, his father and brothers were home from the war.

The main emphasis in the story centers around the impressions made on the boy, predominantly by the blue uniforms which he associates with the "moon":

I can never get the blue of his uniform jacket from my eyes. Not the yellow stripes or the brass buttons, nor the insignia at shoulder and cap are remembered vividly, no. It is that powerful, flashing blue. It seemed immensely superior to the gray of my father and brothers. My father used to say "once in a blue moon" a lot when I was a child. Somehow, the blue of that smart jacket, under which the man's muscles moved and made it glint alive, seemed to have belonged to the man in the moon. That Yankee — the first I had ever seen — was a moon man. A blue — an intensely blue — moon man.[49]

The exaggerated, lurid world of the child is effectively presented in his first-person narrative which includes, among other impressions, that of Amos's "hat with a cockade": "He never wore it that I knew unless for the Sundays when the bishop came to Amelia to preach and then home to dinner with us. Amos wore his hat with the cockade now. I stopped crying just to see that cockade. It was a badge of distinction, a thing that rendered us immune from ordinary things. . . ."[50]

The boy never comments directly about either his mother's bravery or the courtesy of the soldier; he simply describes what happened. He liked to "play store" in his mother's flower garden, and he is there when he first sees the Yankees coming. After they leave, his mother offers her "small embroidery scissors" for him to "sell in his store": "The scissors were forbidden property. I was never to touch them, for mother said the Lord only knew whenever she would get any more."[51] The boy is reluctant to take them, since he does not understand her gesture; but his mother insists, telling him, "We are done embroidering."[52] He hides the scissors in a safe place in the garden where several years later he finds them "under that old stump," recalling, for the boy, the story and the impression made by the man in blue as he "came down the gravel walk between those little button chrysanthemums."[53] The scissors may symbolize his mother's ability to break with their past life of plentiful servants as the time draws nearer for freeing the slaves. It is the boy who, at one point, says to the Yankee, "Amos doesn't want to be free. . . . 'No one does,' the Yankee said . . . 'Nobody is,' my mother said."[54]

The boy's first-person narrative prevents the story's becoming sentimental, for he spends little time telling of feelings. He recalls his fear, and he remembers that, when his mother gave him the scissors, she looked "ready to cry";[55] but he does not dwell on her reaction. He is much like a very young Richard Plume before the Spanish-American War ended and his father's stories began. As the Civil War approaches its end — and Confederate defeat — the boy is not concerned with winning or losing, but with those who are playing the game — their looks, their manners, their uniforms.

Despite the lack of obvious emotion and sentimentality in the story, Stallings gave the subtitle, "A Sentimental Story" to "Gentleman in Blue," but the subtitle is appropriately missing from the renamed "Near Appomattox." A simple story, it is Stallings' only fictional piece written in the first person; and it is the only story he based on a youth of his father's generation. Though I cannot determine whether Stallings is retelling specific family history, his concern for appearance and manners and for the impression these made on the boy are not unlike his attitude toward his own experience or that of Richard Plume. Stallings' return to the past in an objective portrayal of those things fascinating to young adventurous boys reflects a rethinking of a past which had been romanticized to such an extent that he had persisted in a fictional crusade to tell the truth rather than to present stories of "misguided romanticism." Now, he examines youthful impressions which determine later action or participation; and, ironically, the impressions are made by the enemy who only wears a different color. It is as if Stallings, in rethinking his past, is, as Richard Plume had promised, discovering the answer to what had happened to him.

"Gentleman in Blue" is probably not the type of story that the young Stallings heard, for Southern writers at the turn of the century were not likely to treat the Yankee kindly, even in fiction. Young Richard Plume had assumed that Robert E. Lee had won the war until, on a trip to the North, he had learned that "history had been untrue."[56] Stallings seems to be reconsidering what his life might have been like had he not been the victim of his father's and grandfather's misguided romanticism. He recognizes that a child's fascination for costumes (uniforms or cockade hats) is a natural phenomenon in the drama of life, but a "diet of shining swords"[57] in relation to one side only does not prepare one for reality. Furthermore, such distortion adds to the emotional appeal of war, particularly when propaganda — such as atrocity stories — was a great inducement for recruitment during World War I. In "Gentleman in Blue" Stallings concentrates, therefore, on the importance of learning as a child both truth and respect for all men whose only difference may be their costumes.[58] But in his last published new story, "Return to the Woods" (1932), Stallings' maturity encompasses guilt in relation to the duty which binds men.

VI "Return to the Woods"

In "Return to the Woods," Stallings reflects his admiration and understanding for a man who was afraid to fight. His earlier emphasis on courage and on the spirit of the soldier is presented in this simple story of a man ill-prepared for war and well aware of it but capable of courage. In this narrative, two men, a major and an adjutant, return to a French village eight years after the major had "left a foot"[59] there. He brings a wreath "for the cook's grave." As the men approach the "patch," they "feel more like crawling it"; and the major suggests, " 'Let's crawl it again'. . . . The major drops gravely to hands and knees, and he shifts the wreath to his shoulder. Grotesquely, the two men crawled . . . to the garden hedge."[60] They admire the beauty of the woods which "seemed no longer enchanted with the sickly sweet odor of gas and figures of the dead dragged half out of sight along the paths." As they near the garden, they see a woman and child among old apple trees "mothering a dozen new ones":

A fair woman with full breasts was walking the path, a tow-headed baby on her hip. . . . She was anxious to talk. They learned that the garden was ruined. There were too many machine-gun belts and pieces of jagged steel beneath the soil. One was forever turning up brass cartridges in thousands, old steel helmets, and occasional shoes with the small bones of the feet.
    "I think," said the adjutant, "she wants us to clean up the place. I always thought we'd be looked upon as saviors."[61]

They sit down on the steps "of a lodge" and reminisce about the cook. Speaking of the night before battle, the major recalls the cook's request:

"He came to me the night we got up. He said that he was a cook. Not a headquarters cook who could instantly turn into a runner. . . . That he was no soldier. I never heard a man admit so readily that he couldn't stand the pace. Not hysterical, either. As cool as a doctor telling a colleague that he had detected within himself the unmistakable evidence of a fatal malady. 'I just can't go through with it,' he said. 'I just ain't made for this. I'm scared. I'm scared all the time. You'll have to let me go back to the rear and cook for somebody.' . . . He said this as coolly as I repeat it now."[62]

The major, who had sent him to see the doctor, had instructed the cook to "trick his temperature . . . eat soap and throw convulsions . . . do anything to get a ticket to the rear."[63] But, when the cook had repeated to the doctor the same request, the doctor had no choice but to return him to the front "with a whole surgical personnel listening to a man say he was sorry he came to war and would like to go back to a quiet spot and cook potatoes."[64]

When the cook returned, he had crept "into the hole" and had prayed and cried for most of the night. The major recalled taking him to his tent and, on awaking, seeing the cook frying bacon: "He thought he would cook and I would fight. . . . He thought it would be a domestic arrangement. That I would rise . . . and he would have breakfast ready, and then I would shave and go down to the battle. . . . I couldn't do anything. A thousand men ready to die in a wheat field and I would tell one he need not go along? I could not do that. . . . He was afraid of rifles, of firearms generally."[65] Before leaving for battle, they receive a message to "cut the wire." The major recalls giving the clippers to the cook as he promised that he would "be right by him. . . . I said I would see that he got through all right. That it was a duty he owed his friends in the headquarters' detachments to cut the wire for them."[66] And the cook answered, "But I'm a cook."

The major worked from below slashing the wire with a machete, but recalled that the cook "stood upright and cut the wire. I had to stand too. He cut until he was dying. He cut with one hand toward the last. . . . I let him down to the ground when he was through. 'I'm a good cook,' he said. 'Major, I'm a good cook.' "[67]

After finishing his story, the major takes his wreath and begins "walking the road again." The adjutant suggests that they go first to a dram shop for a bottle of wine, but the major responds, " 'This must be done soberly,' . . . As they cleared the wood they looked out upon a plain of crosses in myriads of echelons beneath a tall flagstaff and bravely whipping flag."[68]

The story, "soberly" told, presents a courageous act in a most subtle way. "Recollected in tranquility," the story accents neither courage nor cowardice; it serves as a confession, one foreshadowed earlier in the story by the major's action of dropping on his knees and crawling in the woods. The major admits that he has "never told before" and adds that he "wrote about him the night he was killed"; but "They sent me the ribbons: for me. Beyond . . . extraordinary and all that."[69]

"Return to the Woods" differs from Stallings' earliest fiction in that he reconsiders in it real and psychological problems that he had to cope with during the war, all of which were related to duty.[70] In *Plumes*, he had said, "As for duty, that is the most terrible word of all."[71] In the novel, guilt was associated with Plume's hatred of himself for throwing his life away because of the "tradition persisting among all the Plumes."[72] That Esme suffered also added to his guilt, making him feel "like a criminal"[73] for the life he offered her. In "Return to the Woods" guilt is other-related as Stallings reflects his understanding of the suffering of persons other than himself, as well as his own responsibility for their deaths.

Few who have led men in battle, as Stallings actually did, could have escaped psychological reaction toward the terrible reality of their participation in the deaths of others.[74] It is one thing to cope with one's own physical suffering and the loss of a limb; it is quite another to cope with the guilt of sending young, inexperienced men to their deaths. Some of these reactions and thoughts were probably included in Stallings' later phrase concerning war: ". . . it carries thoughts too deep for tears."[75]

At this point in Stallings' writing career, he seems to have reached a complete understanding of what he called in *Plumes* "why this thing happened to me." True, he had outgrown his Southernness in *Plumes;* and he had recognized in *What Price Glory?* that life was filled with contradictions and absurdities which had meaning only in relation to the way a man plays the game. But Stallings became increasingly concerned in the short stories with man's more admirable qualities such as his capacity for courage, camaraderie, respect, and love, as well as his responsibility to his fellow man with whom he had to share the guilt. He had come to agree with John Donne's feeling that "No man is an island . . . any man's death diminishes me."

CHAPTER 5

Paths of Glory: A World of Paper and Celluloid

I Newspaper Reviews

MANY of Stallings' newspaper articles read like short stories; for, while presenting his facts and quite openly giving his opinions, he tells anecdotes. They also provide important biographical sources of his experience during, and attitudes about war, its heroes, and its novelists. Since I am concentrating on Stallings' shifting and evolving attitudes toward war, I have selected columns in these three categories: reviews (1) of war-related, nonfiction works; (2) of war fiction; and (3) of works on historical heroes.

For my purpose, the most important single article is one written for "The First Reader" on February 8, 1924, the same year that *Plumes* was published and that *What Price Glory?* was produced. A review of Norman Thomas' *The Conscientious Objector in America* (1924), "Paths of Glory" opens with Stallings' defining "a good man" as one who can keep out of trouble "with the least trouble to himself." He extends his definition to include "the good man in war time" as one "who keeps out of war, provided, of course, there isn't some material gain to compensate for his leaving a warm bed to risk his neck." Re-echoing the idea in *Plumes* of going to war to save another man's property, Stallings equates the economic determinant of war with the wars of the Middle Ages; then he writes of "modern war":

In modern war few individuals gain by joining the conflict. Wars are promoted by those who do not intend to join, save for a military caste placed in the rear of the villeins, just as in medieval war, in return for special rewards.

It has become a matter of principle which now causes a man to turn soldier. It is also a matter of principle which causes a man to turn conscientious objector. In America in 1917 both were tarred with the same stick. Both suffered to end war, and both wanted the world to know their principles.

Since war is actually a negation of human principles, it seems to me a damned bad thing to have them in war. Either way you jump — prison or trench — you'll suffer for your principles. The wise man doesn't jump.

Stallings tries to take a middle-of-the-road stance as he considers the absurdity of making either choice. At times, he struggles to show direct sympathy for conscientious objectors, those "alone of all the combatants who have gone undecorated since they lacked a troubadour, a minstrel, to sing of their deeds." Stallings, who applauds Thomas' efforts, considers the work to be "unique among the American chronicles of the brave"; but he adds, "I find the book not without a grim and brutal humor":

These men were against war. So, for that matter, will 10,000 soldiers tell you they were themselves. Each class hated war violently, and I dare say in the end the soldiers more than the objectors. Each was willing to forego freedom of thought and person to protest against it, each in his own way. . . . As to which of these two was of the stouter heart, I cannot determine. Certainly it would seem that the objector, who had no mass thinking to back him, and who had to grope individually for a plan of action, displayed a finer quality of heroism. The advantage, however, pales before not only the willingness but the intention of the other man to die. For, whatever may be the feeling of those about you and those who support you, dying is the most personal and unprecedented thing of all. It has to be done single-handed, whereas even in birth you have your mother to help you.

Stallings tries to be objective; but, like the wounded major of "Esprit de Corps," he reveals his own pride in having participated in the war. He concludes his lengthy article by quoting Shakespeare's Falstaff and by describing him as having the "most admirable, sane viewpoint of the good man who refuses to jump." In response to Prince Hal's "Thou owest heaven a death," Falstaff had responded:

Tis not due yet: I would be loath to pay him before his day. What need I be so forward with him that calls not on me? Well, 'tis no matter; honor pricks me on. Yea, but how if honor prick me off when I come on? How then? Can honor set a leg? No. Or an arm? No. Or take away the grief of a wound? No. Honor hath no skill in surgery, then? No. What is honor? A word. What is that word, honor? Air. A trim reckoning — who hath it? He that died o' Wednesday. Doth he feel it? No. Doth he hear it? No. Is it insensible then? Yea, to the dead. But will it not live with the living? No. Why? Detraction will not suffer it — therefore I'll none of it. Honor is a mere escutcheon, and so ends my catechism.

Stallings' closing comment, which follows Falstaff's speech, is more nearly what one might expect from Captain Flagg or the major of "Esprit de Corps," and it leaves no doubt about his attitude toward Thomas' work: "One pities the conscientious objector, just as one pities the conscientious soldier, but as for giving him vast honor — he that hath it died o' Wednesday."

The total effect of Stallings' comments is quite like the old expression, "I can talk about my own, but no one else can." No individual wants to be reminded that his own actions are wrong, especially if he is suffering physically and psychologically from lessons painfully learned. Men fight to defend the principles they believe in, and they also rationalize in order to continue believing in them. Even if they lose faith in those principles — to the point of admitting it — having those principles questioned by others may appear to be a personal attack. Thus, Stallings, in a sense, defends himself but only to the extent that, while he may not feel like shouting loudly for the warrior, he will do no more than whisper for those who failed to be in the first wave. Characteristics of the younger, unwounded Richard Plume reappear, though faintly.

In the same article, "Paths of Glory," Stallings wrote that ". . . the book needed about the war is one which will tell of the good times back home during the war. . . . It will be a valuable asset against recruiting in the next war. Soldiers should be impressed with the good times of the fellows back home." While not exactly living up to Stallings' concept of the book needed, Arnold Bennett's *Journal* (1932) received Stallings' acclaim because it concerned "mainly his stolid life as a writer of stolid novels in the midst of the great military upheaval of 1914-1918."[1]

Stallings was particularly impressed with Bennett's "honest and pleasant" treatment, without "fanfaronades and flourishes." But he also saw in the work admiration for "men of action":[2] "Quite consciously his journal, the bulk of it, through the war years, shows of what conceited and useless bums the average group of writers is composed when contrasted with men of action. All of them were busy about their little plays and stories — rather eager to hear the fables of returned officers, but not daring to tackle the war as their field and sticking to the old rotation of camilles and bovaries and micawbers, etc. to whack out their so many cents per line."

Stallings' intense resentment of such writers is evident; also, his admiration for the fighting man creeps in — along with one other hint of disappointment: "I was sold on Bennett's first volume, and still remain true on the second, for it hasn't a gilt of bilge in it; not an attitude, not a piece of hate . . . and, to be fair, not a single description of a soldier worth the remembering. Bennett, of all men, lets us down there. Occasionally he describes an officer, but never a man. They were too many peas in a military pod to be worth description."[3] Such treatment of soldiers is the very thing Stallings avoided when he wrote *The Doughboys;* in it, he concentrates on individuals and portrays them with a personal touch.

Stallings' review of John J. Pershing's *My Experience in the World War* (1931) reflects his admiration of the man and the general. Most of the article is devoted to a comparison of Pershing's style with that of other military leaders, but Stallings reveals his delight with the content of the book:

I like his way of setting old Clemenceau crazy and telling Tardieu where to head in: his polite refusal of King George's equally polite request for a casual army or so of American men and his soldierly distrust of Lloyd George tickle the provincial fancy. I like, too, his harassed grin when he perceived that an Italian general had come to ask the loan of just twenty-five divisions to tide him over until the next war. These are good, sound, provincial American stories, and the book is all of a piece with it, with Pershing's native distrust of all gambits European and his conviction that our men should die together or not at all. Clever little people, the Europeans, but they simply did not comprehend.

Stallings takes particular glee in the way that Pershing says what he must say, for Stallings is more concerned with the manner of the soldier than with the war. He seems to view Pershing with as much delight as when he wrote of Sir Henry Morgan in *The Buccaneer* and with some of the same romantic robustness. The tone of Stallings' review of Pershing's work is more in keeping with Stallings' type of humor that appears in such stories as "Turn Out the Guard" and in the later interpretive chronicle, *The Doughboys*, in which Pershing definitely appears as one of the country's great heroes.

Stallings' concern about the failure of others to tell the story of the heroes of his lifetime, the doughboys, is foreshadowed in the article "Relic of the Doughboy Newspaper Embalmed for Our Derision," a review of *Squads Write*, edited by John T. Winterich. A collection of articles selected from *The Stars and Stripes*, the Army newspaper, *Squads Write* provoked Stallings to comment on its "triviality" and its "superficiality of . . . subject matter." Stallings was especially concerned with the lack of truth represented in the selections:

"Reading *Squads Write* one wonders if all reportorial work is so wide of the mark of truth as this is. I think that *Squads Write* is for the most part exceedingly puerile . . . yet redeemed by the fact that most of its staff knew of this puerility."[4] Stallings summarizes his own feelings less objectively:

> . . . reading it now, one is almost moved to tears. Not the tears of an easily invoked ironic contemplation of youth thrown away but tears that the record, day by day, of the many shining and splendid men whose deeds were celebrated herein, is chronicled in such a sorry Iliad, such a cheap silly chanson. . . . Harpers in publishing it may delight hundreds of thousands of ex-doughboys who will receive it with more affection than this reviewer. Myself, when meeting any one of its fine staff again, if I think of their having shared in its editing, can only turn away with the despairing thought that perhaps in no other war in history — this the greatest war of all — was the job of covering it assigned to experts in the trivial.[5]

The deep emotion which Stallings felt for those he later tried to immortalize occasionally appears in just such a column, but rarely does he become so impassioned in his nonfiction. His pride is evinced; he is personally offended by the product; it makes less meaningful his own terrible experience, one seemingly unworthy.

As both a war veteran and a writer, Stallings was naturally interested in other war novels. His favorite, Thomas Boyd's *Through the Wheat* (1923), is often referred to in his reviews of works to which he compares it. For the most part, however, Stallings is primarily the troubadour for unsung veteran writers, such as Captain J. W. Thomason, Jr., and Angus McLeod, former fighting companions.[6] Self-appointed agent for Thomason, Stallings took him to *Scribner's Magazine* which published Thomason's first prose pieces — ones which Stallings praised in "One of Ours," a title he borrowed from Willa Cather. But he was equally impressed with Thomason as "a superb soldier." Battle accounts, at this point, seem to constitute Stallings' favorite reading; and Stallings writes of Thomason's: "His battle accounts, better than Crane's, better than Hugo's, as good as Tolstoi's, are due not only to his superb ability to write and to draw, but chiefly to his amazing feeling for war."[7]

Stallings does not define "amazing feeling for war," but he does relate, with joy, Thomason's preference for action on the sea rather than the sheaf:

> One recalls that Tolstoi says somewhere that never in the literary and artistic crowds of Petrograd and Paris did he ever meet either the men or the

spirit that he found in his early service around Sebastopol. I thought of that the day that Jack Wheeler came to me (I was managing Capt. Thomason as Mr. Kearns does Mr. Dempsey) with the news that he had been to see the work at *Scribner's*, and that Capt. Thomason would have to leave the Marine Corps and take up a long contract, highly remunerative, with Liberty Magazine.

I informed Mr. Wheeler that my champion was not for his stubble; that Capt. Thomason was not desirous of leaving the Marine Corps. "What does he make?" asked Mr. Wheeler. "About $4600." "Good God, that'll never do."

"It'll have to do," I said. "You couldn't get Thomason out of service if you gave him the Chicago *Tribune* and the McCormick reaper."[8]

Stallings especially admires the man, who, free and independent, can pursue such masculine adventure. There is nostalgia in Stallings' description of Marines as he writes:

Thomason is out on the Pacific now, doubtless preparing to win the cup at the winter practice grounds for secondary defense batteries of light ships. . . . But I for one hope that he is making sketches of half-naked marines on the gun deck, brown hides glistening through their white singlets; catching with his marvelous hand the long line of action in the man who holds the lanyard taut for signal, the hunch of the fellow on the platform, the crouch of that one passing the powder charge.[9]

Obviously, the Marines would not all appear alike as had the soldiers portrayed by Arnold Bennett. Stallings' vivid description of Marines is reminiscent of his early portrait in *Plumes* of the healthy Marine, Richard. Indeed, we find a quickening pace and a stepped-up tone of excitement when Stallings writes about Marines. This same enthusiasm for the fighter peaks, for Stallings, in his last work, *The Doughboys*, which includes J. W. Thomason, Jr., in its treatment of men at war.

Stallings may be making an ironic reference to his own protagonist and to himself in his title for a review of James Boyd's *Drums*, "Richard's Himself Again." However, *Drums* (1925) is compared to Winston Churchill's *Richard Carvel* (1925), and Stallings suggests that Boyd has rewritten *Richard Carvel*. *Drums* was Stallings' "pick of the American fiction" for the spring of 1925: "It had been time that a novelist would do the artistic thing by the American Revolution. Such a man would resist either screaming patriotism or bloody irony. Boyd has done it. *Drums* is this reader's pick of the American fiction on the new lists."[10] Stallings, no doubt, thought that this was what he had done in *Plumes*. But, while he had not screamed patriotism, he had definitely presented "bloody irony."

During the latter half of the same year, 1925, Stallings' pick of American fiction was again a war novel — Angus McLeod's *Across the Moon*, for which Stallings said he could "whoop unreservedly." He describes the Scotsman's work as a "must" reading assignment: "The story, a highly erotic thing at points, concerns a young man driven out of his head by war, and his marriage with a chorus girl. I cannot remember anything half so good by any other returned soldier."[11] This favorable comment is but a sample of Stallings' tendency to exaggerate the importance of war works which he particularly likes, such as Leonard H. Nason's doughboy sketches.

Nason was a contributor to *Adventure* whose stories, according to Stallings, "had not been published in permanent form." In "Enlisted Men Only," Stallings admits that "the plots are poor"; but he adds, "who cares?" He especially appreciates Nason's "feeling of the private soldier," a feeling which "saturated" the stories: "None of them will compare in brilliance with Thomas Boyd's *Through the Wheat* as an integrated whole — a feat of narrative perhaps unexampled among other American war books. But these stories should serve throughout time as faithful reproductions of the Yank speech. There is no disillusionment in them. Reading them, one is conscious of Mr. Nason's admiration for those grievous scenes of 1918."[12] Stallings' last two statements accurately describe his own later attitude in *The Doughboys*.

Two other reviews of fiction are worth noting briefly. In "*The Education of Dr. Kerkhoven & Co.*," Stallings comments on the novel's character, Dr. Kerkhoven, who "Became great by reason of opportunities . . . afforded him in the war." But Stallings observes: "This is the popular view that the doctors learned greatly in the war. We know now that the economists learned nothing; that the philosophers learned less; and that the historians retired in even greater confusion. Unless the doctors learned something, that war was simply a lot of pearls cast before a bunch of Bourbons."[13]

By now, 1932, increasingly annoyed that historians had neglected the World War I soldiers, Stallings writes of the fictional Dr. Kerkhoven as if he were human. But he is not really as interested in reviewing the work as he is in telling his own stories about that war, for most of the review is devoted to the real doctor of his story "Vale of Tears." Stallings concludes: "These experiences left me incapable of believing that Dr. Kerkhoven learned a lot in the war. . . . Everybody was crazy in that war."[14]

Though not a review of a war novel, one other article is relevant to Stallings' emerging concepts of reality — specifically, his concern for historical truth. "Aesthete, 1879 Model," is a review of Henry Adams' novel, *Democracy*. Stallings felt that the novel was re-issued because "The Presidential election of 1920, and nothing else, precipitated the demand." Warren G. Harding, a Republican, had defeated Woodrow Wilson; and Harding took office promising a return to "normalcy" after the war years. Stallings explains the relation between the two historical periods:

Adams wrote his work shortly after Rutherford B. Hayes had defeated Samuel J. Tilden . . . and had descended upon Washington with an incompetent troupe of scoundrels and nincompoops. Washington, having survived a great war, was indulging in its customary sneers at European ideas, was running its lobbies full blast, sweating over civil service reforms, thieving from any public opportunities lying about exposed to the mercies of the politicians.

Somehow, in the midst of the recent debacle of the Harding fellowship, it began to be bruited about that the Boston philosopher had once done an anonymous novel which fitted the case all over again. Reading it, one is hugely entertained by the suspicion that his countrymen have altered little in fifty years, and their government . . . not at all.[15]

Of the theme of *Democracy*, Stallings wrote:

The conclusion seems to be that all Governments are bad, all dishonest, all mendacious — as all diplomats in *Democracy* admit freely and with ironic pleasantries. That is, all save the Americans, who boast that theirs is the only simon-pure affair on record. This theme of "Democracy," is hinged upon this false premise, and it is Adams' downright happiness to show that the American is worst of the lot, solely because of his insular hypocrisy in the matter. . . . Few portraits of hypocrites have been more joyfully done. *Democracy* is not a book for the novel reader. It is more likely a volume for those who care for the exceptional, for those who take to such recent action as *A Passage to India* and similar works more devoted to intellectual skill than to narrative gift.[16]

Stallings' open and direct comments about such works as that by Henry Adams represent a man whose admiration for his country did not mean, as he had observed in the "Note" to *What Price Glory?*, giving a sugar coating to things unpleasant. Change comes only with recognition of weaknesses or ills; and Stallings, especially interested in the truth, is even more outspoken in his reviews of works about historical heroes. For example, he reflects in "Drunk with Sacrifice" strong disapproval of Woodrow Wilson in a review of *Robert E. Lee, An Interpretation.* Stallings describes the book's content as an address that Wilson had made in 1909 at the University of North Carolina, "at home in the bosom of his kinsman" where no "George Harvey was . . . Boswell fashion running about to report the doctor's conversation."[17]

Stallings' interest in the work resembles that of a Jamesian scholar reading the biography *Hawthorne* for what it reveals about its author, Henry James. Stallings referred to Wilson's 1909 statements as proof enough for those who still debated Wilson's reasons for entering World War I. And he quotes these lines from Wilson's book: "I wish there were some great orator who could go about and make men drunk with the spirit of sacrifice. I wish there were some man whose tongue might everyday carry abroad the golden accents of that creative age in which we were born a Nation: accents which would ring like tones of reassurances around the whole circle of the globe, so that America might again have the distinction of showing men the way of achievement and hope."[18] Stallings refers to the peace promises of Wilson published before entry into war, but he concludes that Wilson's "statements concerning spilling blood and treasure in order to hold one's self respect" were "not a far jump to eight years later (1917) when a National President, holding a Nation's [respect], talks of spilling blood and treasure for whichever course it seems to him will retain whatever he considers self-sacrifice."[19]

Stallings' attitude toward Wilson was also revealed in his own fiction the same year; in *Plumes*, Richard Plume sympathizes with Wilson only as one cripple to another. He also recalls in a half-conscious state, "The God-damned scoundrelly orators were not there — were not with him."[20] But Esme, as we noted, held Wilson in deepest respect: "It was clear to her that the forces of darkness had encompassed the President about at Versailles. . . . Unlike Richard she had never put her trust in princes, save in dream princes. And she suffered no disappointment when the visit to Paris failed of material settlement."[21] Richard, however, came to disapprove of Wilson's entire crusade. And Stallings increasingly reflects dislike for the man, an attitude that is made more specific in his last work, *The Doughboys* (1963).

In his review-article, Stallings says almost nothing about Lee, despite the fact that Stallings had since childhood been interested in him. However, there is more — exactly one year later — in Stallings' article, "Lee and Jackson,"[22] a review of Major General Sir Frederick Maurice's biography, *Lee the Soldier* (1925). Stallings compares the Major General's technique to that of a Colonel Henderson's in an earlier biography of Stonewall Jackson, for Henderson had responded to Jackson with "inspiration and partisanship," and Stallings laments that General Maurice does not do the same for Lee. Stallings felt that Lee provided "a richer problem for the biographer" than Jackson; and, disappointed in Maurice's treatment, he gave his own opinions about these heroes, disclosing the fact that he had read "every book on Lee . . . " and had relished stories about these heroes: "Lee, the veterans told me, excelled at getting the most boys to the hottest place the fastest. So says Maurice. It is comforting to know that in gaining Southern history at firsthand the one shining tenet of my faith was scientifically accurate."[23]

Stallings' continual preoccupation with war and with its heroes is evident and his admiration for men like Lee or Jackson is explicit: "Only last Tuesday I saw the little white stone hut where his [Jackson's] spirit was received into the bosom of his cruel Fundamentalist God. But Lee endures the cup of defeat and despoilation. (I once had a professor who rode to Washington College where he might sit at the feet of this extraordinary Hannibal after the men had hobbled home from the surrender.)"[24]

Stallings finally concludes that Maurice's biography is "remarkable" only because it "argues what every Confederate veteran has impressed upon every Confederate grandson these sixty years — that Lee was a better man than Wellington or Grant or any of your hammering fellows, and that he holds rank with Alexander and Hannibal and Caesar."[25] Indeed, Stallings considers Robert E. Lee "the great Bayardist of modern times," adding, however, that "he became as remote in the high shining aura of chivalry as Roland himself."[26] The style of this article is filled with allusions to Medieval Romance and to Shakespeare, as was *Plumes*: "Gettysburg, for all its dramatic effect, was a noisy battle where men and horses screamed and bled and fools went their premature ways to dusty death."

Perhaps more realistic and objective than his comments on war fiction, the 1925 review "Lee and Jackson" reflects Stallings' own concern for historical heroes while it also contains his sadness because his faith has been shaken. The "one shining tenet" of his faith remained, however, and for the rest of his life, his favorite topic of conversation was the Civil War and, according to his wife, Robert E. Lee.

II   The First World War: A Pictorial History

Laurence Stallings' technique — an artistic symmetry of beginnings and endings — so beautifully reflected in the five-part structure of *Plumes* — is especially evident in his chronological arrangement of more than five hundred photographs for *The First World War: A Pictorial History* (1933).[27] This work achieves, as Walter Lippmann has noted, "the effect of a great art."[28] Stallings, the dramatist, came to think of the war in terms of a five-act tragedy, and later wrote: "We entered the tragedy at the beginning of the fifth act, like off-stage soldiers in a play; and we entered singing. Woodrow Wilson had given us our simple theme: Kaiser Bill was a villain; and we marched to make the world safe for democracy."[29]

Although the same five-part structure used in *Plumes* is evident in Stallings' design for his pictorial history, he marks no divisions; but he has carefully ordered the pictures to form a classic five-part drama. We might consider the few opening and closing photographs of events — which are separated from the others in time — as the prologue and epilogue. The photographs leading toward war include such scenes as the Congress of Vienna that met in 1815 to re-draw the map of Europe; Bismarck dictating terms of peace to France; a 1906 conference between Germany and France; and headlines announcing the assassination of the heir to Austria's throne. The few postwar photographs in what may be regarded as the epilogue include a photograph of a 1920 execution for those guilty of treason; four photographs of leaders of 1933, Hitler, Stalin, Mussolini, and Kemal Pasha; and two double-page collages which include clippings of statistics about the military forces of nations of the world; such news headlines as "Japan Wrecks League Efforts . . . ," "Roosevelt Warns World to End War, Cut Arms," "Japanese Buy $8,000,000 Arms"; photographs of drilling troops in Japan and Germany, airplanes, tanks, ships — in short, the preparation for World War II.

Within this full circle, which foreshadows a repetition of history, is the main five-act drama — the war — which includes photos representing predominantly Germany, England, France, Russia, and America at war. We see photographs of tourists returning home, reservists parading, banners flowing, posters waving, trainloads leaving — then the first bombardments as Belgian refugees flee, Britain declares war on Germany, and Frenchmen enlist. There are pictures of troop inspections, factories, equipment, ships, parades, propaganda, cartoons, wide-eyed children, raiding parties, ships sinking, and bridges blowing up. There are more enlistments, flags of other nations joining the war, draft boards, troop trains, casualty lists, hospitals, cemeteries, crosses, honor rolls, and, of course, the dead. Nothing has been omitted — and the story is the same for both sides.

On many pages we find the same identification for both enemy and Allies, such as "Oh God Our Help in Ages Past,"[30] the caption for three photographs — a bishop blessing British troops; a priest blessing Russian troops; and a chaplain blessing German troops. There is, occasionally, a borrowed title, such as "Italy: Farewell to Arms,"[31] the caption for a photograph of the dead; and "Return of the Native," the caption of a photo of French refugees returning to their ruins. Sometimes, only a simple turn of the phrase serves for photographs of opposite sides, such as "White victims of the Red Army"[32] and "Red victims of the White Army."[33]

"The Big Parade" is there, but it is represented by a photograph of soldiers packed in "motor lorries" heading for the front.[34] "Plumes" is also there: Kaiser Wilhelm II with his six sons parade — plumes vibrating high in the wind upon their helmets — in Berlin.[35] And opposite this photograph is one of the scattered dead — a picture captioned "No More Parades."[36] A large double-page photograph of the Allies parading through the Arc de Triomphe in Paris is captioned "The Paths of Glory,"[37] and it is placed near the end of the work after photos of the Armistice, followed by photos of coffins, which are captioned "Known" and "Unknown."[38] The honor roll follows, and the fifth act closes. The double-page center photograph for these 298 pages is that of a ruined cathedral in France, captioned "Divine Services."

In Stallings' introduction to the 1933 edition, he wrote that in the anthology there "was no effort to satisfy any special interest." He felt that a "militarist" would be "disappointed by a lack of enough pictures of guns and tactical groups" and that a "pacifist" would not "find enough horror." But the book was reviewed by both pacifists and militarists, and Stallings' growth toward objectivity is demonstrated by the approval the book received from people of such differing backgrounds.

The editors of the *Saturday Review* sent the book for review to

General Peyton C. March, Major General John F. O'Ryan, pacifists Jane Addams and Oswald Garrision Villard, war correspondent Frederic Palmer, and novelists Thomas Boyd, Mary Lee, and Hervey Allen. Generally, they praised Stallings' work.[39] However, novelist Mary Lee describes it as a "journalist's book . . . a work of irony." She wrote:

Each caption is a bit of propaganda. Its name . , . implies a next one. "Here's what you're going to get," it cries to Youth. "See if you like it!" The journalist sets down the facts, gives facts on both sides of a question — and in the process loses all illusions. But the irony of journalism is that no matter how clear the sight of the man who acts as eyes and ears for the public, his disillusion seldom carries over to his readers. They discount truth. They fit the facts to their own prejudices. The men who arranged these pictures were disillusioned men. The captions explain the steps in their disillusionment and not the pictures.[40]

Miss Lee may have confused disillusionment with presenting both sides, but perhaps she was familiar with Stallings' earlier publications. She had, no doubt, recognized particular captions related to his other works. For while the book is predominantly objective — especially in the choice and ordering of photographs — Stallings' personal feelings *are* found in captions to photographs which he described in his introduction as, "some are private." Ironically, this publication was Stallings' last one to include any reference to *Plumes*.[41]

The First World War was an instant success, and it led to a controversy about theories of art between Archibald MacLeish and Malcolm Cowley.[42] MacLeish thought that the book argued "a thesis" and did so "eloquently and unanswerably"; he described it as "one of the most compelling anti-war tracts ever produced. It avoids with a skill which amounts to genius all those flag-waving, drum-beating suggestions which, in the ordinary anti-war book, arouse, in the young, emotions the precise opposite of those intended. And its thesis is a noble thesis — there could be none nobler."[43] But MacLeish was concerned that the reader could look and say, "That is an actual man. He is actually dead. How horrible" — and yet feel none of the horror which Mr. Stallings himself has elsewhere put into a phrase no photograph illustrated. It is possible to turn through the whole book . . . without once recapturing the feel and taste of the time itself, the indelible experience which Mr. Stallings has, in his own office, recalled."

Cowley responded to MacLeish, reminding him, that "It is time for us to admit that you, MacLeish, and I, Cowley, and Hemingway, Wilson, Dos Passos, . . . our relatives who crashed in airplanes or died by machine-gun fire, our friends who were crippled — that all of us fought in vain."[44] Cowley's only "complaint" was that Stallings "could not tell enough of it [truth]."

In "The Dead of the Next War," MacLeish replied to Cowley: "My criticism of Mr. Stallings is not that he should have presented the war of Captain Flagg and Sergeant Quirt, but that in presenting a war from which the dead were deleted, save in their corpses, he presented less than the whole truth. I admit that the presentation of the whole truth might be morally dangerous . . . but as a reviewer of Mr. Stallings' book I could not in honesty ignore the suppression."[45]

Cowley answered:

If the communists answered your nevertheless mephitic outbursts against them with irony and ridicule, would that be propaganda? Of course it would. Propaganda is what the other fellow writes — the attitude to be adopted by our generation toward those whom the War destroyed. Here we come closer to the real issue, yet even here there is no argument between us which cannot be resolved by definition. We differ chiefly in emphasis. . . . And this can be proved by what we remember about any of those . . . who died so uncomplainingly. . . . They were good guys . . . and they entered because it was the right thing to do and partly because they felt a physical need for danger. But danger has a way of justifying the cause for which it is endured. Our friends soon became patriots . . . they marched to the front convinced that they were fighting for democracy. . . . And however they felt about it, they were killed. Patriotism, love of danger, fear, boredom, disgust — all the things that went on inside their heads didn't matter. . . . What shall we say of them now? . . . We can judge their deaths subjectively or objectively. . . . The real issue between us is, How shall we regard the dead of the next war? . . . We may even come to share the illusions of the dead, and we shall in any case defend the system which makes the next war as inevitable as tomorrow. . . . What are you doing to prevent that war before it is too late? I ask you this as an editor, a man, a poet or anything you please.[46]

Cowley's response reflects an understanding as well as an appreciation of Stallings' attitudes and purposes. But even more important as far as Stallings' preoccupation with war is concerned is Kenneth Burke's treatment. Burke used Stallings' work and the MacLeish-Cowley debate as his point of departure for a consideration of the poet's contradictory response, one best represented in war literature. Burke felt that it "was highly questionable whether the true subject of *The First World War* was an actual war at all. I think that Cowley is more nearly correct on this point, since he is concerned with our responses to the possibility of war rather than . . . to a war already gone into history."[47]

Referring to MacLeish's concern for Stallings' presentation of the repellent side of war, Burke admitted that the artist had to select his material "out of the past and the present. . . . For the poet, not all of such material is confined to objective events. Much of it lives in the memory, emphasis, interests, preferences, and apprehensions of his contemporaries." He asks of MacLeish, however, ". . . does he not himself grow absolutist in assuming that the War possesses one definite, absolute character which must remain unchanged throughout history? . . . If our relationship to war is different now from what it was in 1916, why must we attempt to uphold, by strange canons of 'truth' the 1916 character of war?"[48]

Burke agreed, however, that man usually responds with contradiction and that exposure to the repellent may "partially close the mind to the repellent" since overexposure to "pro" anything can produce "anti" attitudes and vice versa. Burke then summarizes what he calls the "Bohemian-practical; the useful-sacrificial; the militaristic-pacifistic" with the following theory: "I believe that a kind of egoistic-altruistic merger can be established whereby a man may be found honestly devoting himself and sacrificing himself to activities which are primarily pursued because they net him large profits. . . . If one possesses a resource or device that greatly sustains or protects him, he will even risk his life to keep it or improve it."[49]

Burke's theory helps shed light on Stallings' lifelong concern with war and on the fact that all his major publications dealt with that subject. Both egoistic and altrustic elements are represented in his career. Belleau Wood was a terrifying experience; but, in using it as fictional and dramatic material, he also found it a useful experience. And, while it altered his life considerably by removing him from, yet forcing him into, different "tourneys" of the world, his memories of that experience sustained and protected him as he continued to devote and sacrifice himself to it. This factor may help to explain his worldwide pursuit of war as a war correspondent in 1935 and his re-enlistment in 1942, but it also helps to explain the attitudes he represents in *The First World War*. At this point in Stallings' career, Harlan Hatcher wrote of Stallings: "Taking his work in all forms as a single whole, Laurence Stallings has done more than any one American author to cut away the romantic glamour of war and to expose its wretchedness."[50]

III   *War Correspondent in Ethiopia*

In 1935, Stallings headed a news, newsreel, and newspaper expedition to Ethiopia to cover the Italo-Ethiopian War. Sponsored by Fox Movietonews and the North American Newspaper Alliance, Stallings took along a fleet of motor trucks, four cameramen, and a supply of American flags — for protection.[51] Newspapers throughout the country carried his dispatches in which he evinces both a fascination for the challenge of his assignment, and feeling for those he covers.[52]

The earliest articles are long, and they reflect Stallings' excited anticipation of what lies ahead in such comments as this one: "All over Europe the diplomats, getting out their fire-hats for the first time since 1914, are blinking at Mussolini's dazzling successes."[53] Equally revealing is this statement: "Though the Ethiopian warriors are ignorant of recent developments, they know that a fight is looming, and they shout their 'hallelujahs' as they travel toward the front with water bottles, bed sheets and bayonets and, when occasion demands, bearing army trucks over their heads."[54]

Stallings includes some vivid descriptions of the leaders, particularly Wehib Pasha, the Turkish chief of staff of an Ethiopian army. He nicknames, affectionately, this leader "Eagle Beak" and describes him as "resplendent in his red-gold fez and Turkish trappings,"[55] a description that may recall the boy's fascination with the cockade hat in "Gentleman in Blue." Wehib Pasha also represents "fury incarnate directing an army of Christians and Moslems against a common foe," a description which bears some allusion, perhaps, to the Medieval Romances of the Crusades.[56]

While the information Stallings had received before arriving in Ethiopia assured the Italians a "speedy victory," Stallings, after considering Ethiopian Emperor Haile Selassie's choices of submission or subjugation, wrote: "As to the possibility of conceding to the Italians any of the Ethiopian plateau — one would as soon expect the French to give up Normandy." Though Stallings exaggerated in this statement, he was, at the time, seeing only one side. His articles are filled with praise for the Ethiopian "warriors" unschooled in modern military tactics, whom he describes as "real fighters. . . . Personally, this correspondent cannot believe that Ethiopia's cake will be cut in our time. The writer has seen enough in the last two weeks to convince him that the occupation and pacification of Ethiopia would bankrupt any government interested in it."[57] He especially admired the Ethopians' spirit of nationalism, the more so because of the un-equal odds — the challenge, the risk — as they struggled for sur-vival.

He includes one interesting account of his own involvement with Ethiopia's military, describing their shock when "civilized war" finally began:

I was awakened by the lamplight streaming into my quarters, and, in the doorway stood an Ethiopian Colonel. He begged me to arise and to tell the world that the Italians were bombing a Webbe Shibeli village, killing not troops but women and children.

After weeks of probing his hopeless taciturnity, the spectre of the Colonel's sad face made me realize how much these people understood the world; how much they thought of a battle in the sense of man-to-man con-flict; how greatly they must now suffer because they remained isolated in the midst of modernity while devoting themselves to the chains of feudalism and slavery.

I realized that the Colonel's visit was an effort at propaganda to involve the world in Ethiopia's defense when he said: "The government at Addis Ababa is requesting all journalists to tell the nations of the world that the Italians are making war on women and children. There are plenty of targets in the Webbe Shibeli area, but the Italian planes deliberately sought out the civil population." Ethiopia now begins her course in modernity with the end not in sight. This country, so beautiful, so savage, and so ignorant, stands aghast at the horrors of "civilized warfare."[58]

Ironically, at the same point in time, Stallings was being asked to describe generals as men who "made little boys sleep in graves." He could only repeat the request, recognize its propagandistic purpose, and remain as objective as he could among out-numbered, out-modernized warriors. But he is sympathetic and, at the same time, sad. No doubt, the use of modern war tactics was a stark reminder of the horror he had once endured — a reminder which rendered the war game less fascinating.[59]

IV "The War to End War"

Stallings came out of retirement to publish in 1959 "The War to End War," much of which is included in his last publication, *The Doughboys* (1963). In this article, Stallings remembers, with nostalgia and without bitterness, those prewar days of idealism and the simplicity of the war itself when compared to the complexity of World War II:

A generation freshly memoried in the deeds of the Second World War cannot appreciate the simplicity of the first one. A brilliant defense at Chateau-Thierry, some fine bolstering counterattacks in the intervening two months before the reduction of Saint Mihiel, and the great grinding sacrifices of the Argonne: that was the tale. It was told by correspondents still of the Richard Harding Davis tradition: it had no simple chroniclers such as Ernie Pyle. The result was that, when the men came home and began to write realistically of their experiences, the public was shocked as literary and dramatic works that seem, at this far-off date, rather pale by contrast with the works that followed the later war. . . . In both wars there was beyond the death and the mutilation, the heroism and sacrifice, an American feeling of idealism. The literature following the wake of both wars would deny this; writers try to single out the variation from the norm. The coward seems more interesting, in pedestrian literature, than the heroic figures chosen, say, by the Greeks in their great age. Even the films following the first war that were concerned with the gallantries of the aviators will show . . . that it is the boy who is frightened who holds the interest of the writer.[60]

Apologetic for those postwar disillusioning works, Stallings felt that "in its way, the First World War left no great works . . . nothing like the work that Tolstoi, a generation after it, created from the wreck of Napoleon's dream; nothing like Stendhal's description of the field of Waterloo in *The Charterhouse of Parma*. Yet the men who returned from the first one were unhampered, uncensored; above all they were victorious. They could not set down, however, their deepest feelings about it, any more than could the men who shook hands at Appomattox."[61]

Stallings, the aging warrior who had transcended in the intervening years since World War I his earlier disappointment and bitterness, records his confession with this conclusion: "Thomas Mann says somewhere that nothing is so remote, so difficult to recapture, as the immediate past. It must be that way with our First World War. The men who fought it are grandfathers, their own sons recalling a far more complex affair. And no anthologist can ever bring back the full body of it; though like all wars it carries thoughts too deep for tears."[62]

Stallings' reference in 1959 to "anthologist" may have been an allusion to Hemingway whose *Men at War* was reissued in 1955 and included "Vale of Tears." But Stallings' attitude toward fiction had changed during his years of retirement. In a letter of June 28, 1960, to Professor H. Edward Richardson, Stallings wrote of his disillusionment with fictioneers. He referred to his, by now, more famous contemporaries, Hemingway and Faulkner:

Hemingway suffers because, in his inherent modesty, he pictures his hero as Hemingway, but without the rough instinct of the born killer. Faulkner, of course, is only good with his caricatures, such as the poor-white Snopes' family. He falls flat with the Sartoris outfit, knowing them to be archaic, phony XVIIth century posturers, and yet somehow clinging to the notion that he has sublimated his own pretensions to nobility. There is nothing new about that: witness Shakespeare homing to Stratford and building New Place to live like an Alderman, bitter, ugly, miserably unhappy.

Stallings explained his preference for "the works of Sir Julian Huxley and the Scientific Humanists":

Sir James Fraser, when he ended "The Golden Bough" had followed the course of magic to Contagious Magic,* through primitive religions to ritualistic ones, and knew that the Scientists were now lying in the weeds. He believed that the Religion of the Scientists would, in its turn, be replaced by something not yet within our ken. Einstein died despairing because he did not know what this was: there was no writer to tell him. Meanwhile I read these people faithfully: H. Bedford Jones, the Astronomer Royal; George Gamow, who helped Edward Teller over his mathematica lacunae; George Gaylord Simpson, the Harvard bone man; and above all, Theodore von Weidsacker of Bonn, who has revived old Kant's hypothesis. They are the only kind of writers who make no pretenses of not knowing. The fictioneers, as Edward Teller says, *all lack imagination. . . .*

At this time, Stallings, when urged by his friend Max Wyeth of Harper and Row, began research for his interpretive history of the American Expeditionary Forces of World War I, *The Doughboys.*

CHAPTER 6

Tragedy and Triumph:
The Doughboys

I *Structure, Style*

THE six parts which comprise *The Doughboys* (excluding
Prologue and Epilogue) are Part I — "June, 1917-June,
1918: Build-up"; Part II — "June 1-July 15, 1918: Desperation";
Part III — "July 18-August 12: Counterattack"; Part IV — "August
8-September 26; Offensive, First Phase"; Part V — "September 26-
October 14; Offensive, Second Phase"; and Part VI — "October 15-
November 11: Offensive, Final Phase."[1]

"Build-up" is the story of "the first arrivals" (subtitled "*Nous
voilà, Lafayette!*") in France and of chaotic attempts at organiza-
tion. The opening section includes such stories as "The Education of
Private Bailey" and "Practice at Cantigny." Battles at Belleau Wood
and Vaux make up Part II, "Desperation"; and the progress of the
war at Soissons provides the bulk of material for Part III,
"Counterattack." "Offensive, First Phase," Part IV, centers on the
men who fought at Saint-Mihiel and on the birth of the First
American Army, which continues its progress in "Offensive, Second
Phase," Part V, as the war draws closer to an end. "Offensive, Final
Phase," Part VI, includes stories of the battles at Meuse-Argonne
and Sedan; and it concludes with a brief summary of the casualties
of the war: "The Doughboys buried only eighty-three thousand
casualties. . . . There was no stillness on the Yank fighting lines, as
at Appomattox. It was a matter of noisy laughter, of men too weary
to shed tears."[2]

In the Prologue to his work, Stallings pondered about his reason
for writing the work: "Why write of them at this hour? Why open
the door of a room sealed off in my mind for many years? I chose to
walk among these buddies of the past so that they may be
remembered. There was never an official history written of them. No
anthologist has brought back the full savor of their ignorance or their
valor, of their ultimate skill."[3]

When he comments briefly on what has been omitted, he states that he "avoided the stories of those whose loss hurt . . . the most. . . ."⁴ He summarizes his aims in the following paragraph:

I sing not so much of arms, which the Doughboy mainly borrowed, as of the man himself, conscious of being unable to summon him back in entirety, and heartsick of enduring the melancholy of trying to recover long buried remembrances of things past, of those who, in the phrase of Captain Cyril Falls, "were denied long life." I have avoided, too, as much as possible, the traits of the professional historians, who would instantly recognize me for an armchair imposter; but I must occasionally sketch the big picture, and can only hope that readers will find my chronicle designed to be read and remembered, and not studied.⁵

As a kind of latter-day troubadour for those vanishing heroes, Stallings relates the story of the American Expeditionary Forces. Epic-like in that it centers heroically on the doughboy as the predominant and singular hero of a series of great achievements, the work includes something of everything, which adds to the expansiveness of its panoramic presentation. Complete with historical data (statistics, charts, maps, catalogues of divisions, photographs,) as well as collected stories from friends, diaries, memoirs, autobiographies, and records, *The Doughboys* represents Stallings' final effort to recapture the full flavor of the time as no anthologist had done. He concentrates on personal details as he refers, by name, to one commander, then another, or to one doughboy after another. The reader gets to know such people as General John J. Pershing, Lieutenant General Robert L. Bullard, Major General Hansom E. Ely, Sergeant Alvin York, Sergeant Charles E. Reilly, Corporal Leo J. Bailey, and many more.

But Stallings emphasizes the story of the less-known doughboy as he relates many brave acts, and he records them as if they had recently occurred. But he is in retrospect more enthusiastic: he draws exciting, live portraits that a historian could not. For Stallings, the man-artist, uses his total experience as he combines his literary talents with a lifelong knowledge of books, men, and war. He understands the confusion which resulted from Pershing's determination to hold American troops together rather than intersperse them among the Allies. He moves, camera-like, to Cantigny and on through Belleau Wood, Vaux, Soissons, Saint-Mihiel, Meuse-Argonne, Blanc Mont, and, finally, Sedan. But he takes the reader for close-ups of the front lines, the kitchens, the hospitals and, on inspection tours, to small villages — almost everywhere.

He includes stories of the mistakes made, the casualties which resulted, the jealousies among the high command, the competitions, the battles and their results. All of this material is presented in a variety of styles as he recaptures, heroically, the past. For example, Stallings the essayist writes: "When the French launched their Nivelle offensive, their mission in Washington, headed by Marshal Joffre, had asked for no American troops. They did not think Americans would be trained in time to affect a situation which would find dozens of German divisions returning from the Russian front."[6]

But Stallings the conversationalist says: "The arrival of *les americains* was like a sudden burst of noisy roisterers into the truce of the family fireside. Every man in the 1st Division wanted to go on a patrol, and then a raid; each wanted to kill a German, to capture one, to be the first. If not the first in the A.E.F. then he wanted to be the first in the whole damn division, or brigade, regiment, battalion, company, platoon, squad."[7]

In contrast, we have Stallings the poet: "It was beautiful country, rolling hills and clumps of larches and poplars screening the small villages with their wisps of smoke from chimney pots — quiet, serene, unscarred by heavy warfare."[8]

But Stallings is also the dramatist, who places his singular stamp on a piece of dialogue; and the ring is clear, authoritative: "Private Charles MacArthur, sent on a blistering errand to an . . . Alabama battery . . . inquired . . . where he might find the first sergeant. 'Yank, this battery ain't never had no goddamn top sergeant and ain't never going to stand for none.' "[9]

And there is Stallings the naturalistic humorist: "It was four days before their company had a hot meal . . . and the survivors subsisted on horsemeat until O'Connor . . . acquired some French rolling kitchens and large stocks of corned-beef hash . . . for a mulligan stew. 'Why're ya makin' so much hash, Sergeant? There's only fifty-nine of us left!' 'Listen, buddy, hash ain't no orchid that has to be worn the same day!' "[10]

We also find the reporter Stallings: "The 37th poet was a national figure, the sports writer Grantland Rice. At the age of thirty-nine he had enlisted in New York City as a private in the United States Army, converting his $75,000 assets into cash and entrusting it to a New York lawyer to invest for his wife and their . . . daughter."[11]

And Stallings, the defender, asserts: "The general impression of Americans was that the colored soldier was mainly a comic figure, incapable of undergoing danger over long intervals. The Harlem boys were the first to wipe out that impression. As for being comics, they were natural humorists gifted by God Almighty, deliberately sending their officers into gales of laughter; but the loss of fifteen hundred men in 191 days in the zone of fire was not a laughing matter."[12]

He gives this brief treatment of the forming of the "92nd (Negro) Divison . . . the first of its kind" in American history:

Its formation had been regarded by the Army as political dynamite. . . . Actually it had been the result of suggestions by philosophers and humanitarians, such as Joel Spingarn of Columbia University. Spingarn would have approved General George S. Patton, Jr.'s attitude in a later war. When Patton received his first Negro division, grapevine had it that General Eisenhower, a soldier faultless in his regard for minority groups, had sent an officer from his staff to brief Patton on the advisability of never referring to the racial background of his new regiments. The Green Hornet, who was a fighter incarnate, was said to have addressed his newcomers as follows: "Well men, I am happy to have you here. I don't give a damn what color you are, just so you kill those sons-of-bitches in the green suits.[13]

In addition to references to a later war and its heroes, Stallings, as a student of history and war, offers an occasional glimpse at previous heroes. Of Jackson, he writes: "Andrew Jackson would have made Sergeant York postmaster at Nashville on the spot, throwing some stay-at-home rascal out of office."[14] He reflects admiration in his explanation of the naming of the 30th Division, made up of National Guard troops from South Carolina, North Carolina, and Tennessee: "Since Andrew Jackson had been born in the first state, mixed his law studies with cockfighting, drinking and gambling in the second, and won immortality in the third, they called themselves 'The Old Hickory Division.' "[15]

There are, of course, references to Robert E. Lee and Stonewall Jackson: "There have been various cacklings about tactics in the Meuse-Argonne series of battles, some commentators going so far as to class them with Grant's battering of Lee before Petersburg. Both points are poorly taken. Grant was fixing the attention of Lee, the cream of the Confederate team; but Liggett had no General the Honorable Sir William Tecumseh Sherman ripping out the guts of the Rhineland."[16]

He describes the failure of Major General Clarence Edwards to "push forward at all cost . . . to the railroad Nanteiul — Chateau-Thierry" at Liggett's command, concluding with, "Grant would have relieved him; Sheridan would have cursed him out of head-quarters, Stonewall Jackson would have put him under arrest. The Iron Commander bided his time."[17]

Stallings, the friend, includes his own, such as "Second Lieutenant Roland H. Neel, aerial observer of the 99th Aero Squadron, who had, with his pilot, won the Distinguished Service Cross a month earlier for completing an observation mission and scattering an enemy infantry company around Saint-Die after control wires had been shot away and Neel had pushed and pulled the several cables with his hands.[18]

And Stallings, the realist, includes items excluded from official documents such as slogans ("The official slogan of the Harlem boys, never printed on official documents, was 'God Dam, Le's Go!' ")[19] and songs. Including one of the verses from *Mademoiselle From Armentières*, he relates the events that led to a "new series of verses"[20] as he recaptures the full flavor of the time.

The playwright Stallings includes pages of dialogue between Pershing and Foch,[21] but it is primarily the storyteller who makes lively reading of this chronicle that is no "silly chanson," no "sorry Iliad": Writing of Lieutenant Frank Luke, the "Texas Balloon Buster," who performed "the finest feat of any American aviator,"[22] Stallings relates this story:

His hatred of enemy balloons and of the havoc they might direct upon the Doughboys was a consuming passion. The remotest regard for his own safety was never present in Frank Luke. . . . Luke set out alone to destroy two German gas bags. Approach was always perilous; the balloon company was surrounded by skillful machine gunners and antiaircraft cannon, often with pursuit planes ambushed in the sun. . . . Luke destroyed his first balloon on his first pass, and was immediately aware of three enemy aircraft hovering beyond, and waiting for him. He went for them head on, shooting down two Fokkers, while the third airplane took evasive action. When Luke turned to pursue he realized that by changing course slightly he could pass at the second balloon. This he made successfully, shooting it down in flames. He then pursued and destroyed the third German airplane, an A.V.G. observation craft, though six American Spads were moving on it.

He was a golden boy, with an unequaled record of fourteen victories in eight days, with five victories in eight minutes. The gods loved him; but he did not have to die young. He chose death himself after he disappeared from the sky as mysteriously as had Georges Guynemer, the consumptive youngling of fifty-six victories, who was the hero-genius of the French nation. . . . Thin air seemed to have taken both these lads aloft to some, and more benign, sky; but the inquisitive Captain Merian C. Cooper . . . returned from captivity . . . to discover Frank Luke's fate. He found the rusting engine, the skeleton of fuselage, and he found his friend's grave. The boy had been wounded and downed behind German lines, had leaped out and with his Colt 45 shot it out with a patrol seeking to take him prisoner, standing at bay and dying with his boots on, Texas style, taking others with him to eternity.[23]

The work is filled with anecdotes about individual heroes as Stallings recalls, with admiration, the *men* of World War I.[24] "The Doughboys were fighting for their own pride of manliness,"[25] Stallings wrote — and he wrote about them for much the same reason. He is much more modest when he refers to the "officer with the Idaho willow foot who led that first wave" at Belleau Wood.[26] At age twenty-three, and not knowing whether "he was a second lieutenant, a first lieutenant, or a captain in the expanding Regular Line," he was "gas-sick . . . had a piece of steel in his left leg, and did not care":

Having lost a spiral legging while crawling, he had cut his left breeches leg short, and his beautiful forest-green uniform was held together with strings. He still wore his Sam Browne, spit-shined to conceal his cowardice in having to wear it, and his Colt 45, cocked, was stuffed into his shirt front. . . . On reaching the rifle pits the gas-sick boy jumped in and began fighting his way from pit to pit, diving headfirst over the undug links. . . . The young officer took nine men, leaving the rest to hold the curve, and moved west by south, now out of the woods. He did not last two hundred meters. Awaiting him were about 150 troops of the counterassault teams, untouched by the bombardment. Half an hour later, well tourniquetted, he sat up and gave Major Ralph Heyser of the leapfrog battalion their exact position, and soon heard the shouts, shots, and screams of the mopping up.[27]

In sharp contrast to the wounding which Richard Plume recalled as he sped to Walter Reed Hospital, this passage is, to my knowledge, the only autobiographical record of Stallings' wound. We find no disillusionment in it — though, ironically, Stallings' second leg was amputated in 1963, the publication year for *The Doughboys*. He can recall his "beautiful" green uniform, whereas in *Plumes* "green" for Richard was always associated with things nauseous or gaseous (gangrenous).[28]

The only lines which hint of deep grief are those which close his story of the World War I doughboys: " 'I saw battle-corpses,' Walt Whitman had written after another war, '. . . myriads of them, and the white skeletons of the young men, I saw them, I saw the debris and the debris of all the slain soldiers of the war, but I saw they were not as I had thought, they themselves were fully at rest, they suffered not, the living remained and suffered, the mother suffered, and the wife and the child and the musing comrade suffered, and the armies that remained suffered.' " From Whitman's elegy to Abraham Lincoln, *When Lilacs Last in the Dooryard Bloom'd*, the lines appropriately conclude a work which, in a sense, eulogizes the doughboys as they have once more passed in review.

In his Epilogue, Stallings concludes with a recorded conversation that occurred between General Pershing, the "Iron Commander," and Stallings' friend Captain John W. Thomason, Jr., aboard the *U.S.S. Rochester*, which, in 1923, carried the General to South America "as a political emissary of Calvin Coolidge."[29] Thomason invited Stallings to lunch "the noon before Pershing was to come aboard"; and, after Thomason had returned from that trip, he told Stallings what Pershing's last words had been: "They never knew they were beaten in Berlin . . . it will all have to be done all over again."[30] Stallings, the next year (1924) in *Plumes*, had echoed these words. His brief recollection in *The Doughboys*, however, is the only statement that in any way resembles statements made in his novel of disillusionment. Placed in the context of a recorded conversation for *The Doughboys*, the lines no longer have their earlier meaning.

There is at least one attitude, however, found in *The Doughboys*, which had not changed since *Plumes*: Stallings' opinion of Woodrow Wilson. Of him Stallings wrote, "Few even now realize that America was never a member of the Allies. Woodrow Wilson was so fiercely self-centered he would join with no one, not even his loyal opposition at home, in any of his dreams."[31] But Stallings' indignation toward Wilson seems to be largely because of Wilson's attitude and action toward the fighting men:

Woodrow Wilson . . . seems to have set the tone for an historical limbo by his conduct when he reached Paris and the Peace Conference. Only an hour away was Chateau-Thierry, where a West Point lieutenant with his army of fourteen Doughboys . . . had dashed across the wagon bridge to begin the last-ditch defense of Paris. A right turn and a five-mile spin could have brought the President to the railroad embankment at Mezy, where Ulysses Grant McAlexander's 38th Infantry slaughtered a brigade of Prussian Grenadiers. A left turn for the same distance and Mr. Wilson would have stood by the hunting lodge in Belleau Wood. Or, proceeding north by west to Picardy, he might have been in the village square where the 1st Division opened the ball at Cantigny. . . . But he seemed reluctant to face any of the scenes of the battles his acts had brought about, however noble his motives must have been. It was as if some camper had left a careless fire, and was loath to view the blackened stumps of a once verdant wood.[32]

Slighted, along with thousands of others, by the Commander-in-Chief of America's armed forces, Stallings, a former Marine and a man of pride, could not forgive the President's error of omission.

II *Reviews*

The reviews of *The Doughboys* were generally favorable — some enthusiastic. Eldridge Colby, for *Best Sellers*, applauded Stallings' efforts and called the section on Belleau Wood "a classic. . . . Stallings has recreated for us the enthusiasms and the determinations of those days. He has told of the events as they went by, always with an eye toward the interesting and the human. He has done it with patriotism. He has also done it with emphasis on the personal."[33] For *Saturday Review*, Mark L. Watson summarized his approbation of a chronicle written "with a soldier's hot admiration for gallantry and fortitude" in this way:

Here is a grand mingling of men and deeds and qualities that make history, as they do drama — the tragic and the comic, the drab and the picturesque, the frolicsome and the rough, a long and losing struggle suddenly turned to success and vice versa, tension suddenly relieved by lighthearted interruption — with all action moving irresistibly toward the final curtain. Very far indeed from an official history, *The Doughboys* is a tale so moving that one can hardly lay it aside until it is finished.[34]

Alistair Horne found Stallings' descriptions praiseworthy, particularly those of Belleau Wood, Chateau-Thierry, St. Mihiel, the Argonne, and the St. Quentin Tunnel. But he also appreciated accounts of such heroes as Pfc. Dillboy and Sergeant York. The most interesting part for him, however, was Stallings' portrayal of "General 'Black Jack' Pershing: a reserved, granite-hard figure — the opposite of all that his Allied colleagues expected an American general to be — whose highest tribute to a soldier was to call him 'a fighter . . . a fighter . . . a fighter,' and who could yet distress a battalion hot out of battle by inquiring about the V.D. rate."[35] Stallings' admiration for "Bayardists" such as Lee and Jackson no doubt colored his presentation of the "Iron Commander," General John J. Pershing.

With *The Doughboys*, Stallings' literary career came full circle and so did the man. But it is a long journey from the fictional "chronicle" of *Plumes* to the historical chronicle of *The Doughboys*. None of the chronicle's many real characters in any way resemble Richard Plume, who, guided by the fictional publication, *The Wounded Doughboy*, took part in a pacifist movement. The absence of the word "wounded" in the title of Stallings' final publication may best represent, structurally, the reversal of Stallings in attitude toward life as well as his selection of the genre for his expression of that attitude. For history is, or should be, based on truth; but fiction is a product of the imagination; and imagination, for Stallings, played strange tricks when, as a boy, he became captivated with the romance of war.

Conclusion

IN *Plumes* and in "The Big Parade," Laurence Stallings expresses his disillusionment with a war that meant not only literal death but, in a sense, death for the living who withdrew to contemplate personal loss. War was impersonal; it dehumanized; it was absurd. These attitudes continue in *What Price Glory?*, where the disillusionment is tempered with humor as Stallings treats, in a tragi-comic form, the clash of oppositions represented in war and in life in order to reflect a concern for the mystery of something which could be both horrible and fulfilling. But there was camaraderie in the play that was not in the novel. As Stallings juxtaposes seriousness and buffoonery in the play, he presents with frank admiration the courageous men who could adapt to the absurdities and who could play games with the cards of death.

In *First Flight* and in *The Buccaneer,* Stallings' fascination with adventure centers on the masculine historical hero; and he treats romantically those who did not fear death. And in "Esprit de Corps," in which death is subordinated, Stallings responds with pride in his corps when a spirit of healthy competition among the wounded men helps them cope with a singular reality. But it is in "Vale of Tears" that the camaraderie of the wounded, male world shows itself in codes based on consideration and respect. Disillusionment is replaced by a kind of transcendent affirmation as Stallings, with pride and without sentimentality, recalls the long hospital experience.

Humor and satire conjoin in "Turn Out the Guard," and Stallings becomes increasingly objective. We find less about the horrors of war as he considers, laughingly, some of the absurd competition it produced among men devoted to petticoat power. And in "Gentleman in Blue" he reconsiders the impressions war made on a boy who, like many, is normally fascinated with the display of uniforms and cockade hats, rather than with the horror of war.

The last published story, "Return to the Woods," is an objective remembrance of the brave. In a confessional mode, Stallings pays tribute to one lieutenant whose duty renders him helpless to spare another man from death. Stallings' increasing concern for man's responsibility, which inevitably produces guilt about the suffering of one's fellowman, is reflected in a less self-centered attitude toward the wounds inflicted by war and by life. This more mature attitude doubtless influenced his objective editorial selection of photographs, his arrangement and subtitles, that present both sides in *The First World War: A Pictorial History;* but a few captions continue to tell his personal grief.

In the newspaper articles, Stallings reflects mainly pride and admiration for his and others' heroic participation in World War I, as he tells — at times, with nostalgia — anecdotes of the brave; but he also reflects his own disapproval of the historians, the editors — as well as the President — who had slighted the fighting men. Retaining a faith in such "ancestral" leaders as Lee and Jackson who had fought with their men, Stallings becomes less proud of his bitter response in *Plumes* and more determined to write about the doughboys' heroic efforts. He explains apologetically in "The War to End War" the difficulty of recapturing the immediate past, particularly an event whose legacy was, for his life at least, "thoughts too deep for tears."

In *The Doughboys,* then, he celebrates the heroic efforts of the men who fought World War I — though his attitude toward Wilson had not changed. Wilson had been no "Bayardist" as had Lee or Jackson. Equally proud, however, of all those who had participated, Stallings tells with devotion their story — making heroes of them all.

Stallings' boyhood fascination for such things as competitive and risky games, parades, battles, uniforms, cockade hats, and heroes seems always to have been part of him. It influenced his actions as a young adult seeking glory and recognition on the football field. It was another long, but natural, step to become a Marine on the battlefield, an adult attracted to danger. This early preoccupation, directly related to romanticized versions of history, contributed little to his ability to cope with the reality of war, which ultimately cost him his legs. But the loss, ironically, led to an understanding of the price he had paid for truth. Rebelling against misguided Romanticism, Stallings adopted, almost obsessively, a concern for truth as he began in *Plumes* his own crusade to attack what he took to be the source of his Byronic folly, his martial madness. Stallings reacted with bitter disillusionment to a war which denied him a mobility related to masculinity. For a man whose moments of glory had been defined through action on a football field, Stallings' responses to war and to life were directly related to — indeed, inseparable from — his wound.

In *Plumes*, he had seen all things as wounded. He had presented a Naturalistic view of man, a victim of chance, who had to cope with a life which was essentially absurd. The pomp and show, the plumes of life, were diminished; romance was destroyed; and only the cold, hard scientific fact that economic determinism was one of the inevitable controlling fates of life was left. Further, he felt that life was filled with contradictions or oppositions which often clashed inexplicably, absurdly, with each other. These oppositions he reflected in the tragi-comic play *What Price Glory?*, where he represented man as an adaptable animal who, despite his wounds, automatically struggled for survival. The struggle, directly related to competition, made sense only in the way a man played the game; it had meaning only in the relationship of one soldier to another, or more broadly, of one person to another. For man cannot play the game alone.

Games imply codes; and, while all the codes in *Plumes* were denied as courtly and outmoded traditions, codes became associated in the drama and the short stories with respect for human feelings — not with superficial behavior. Thus, Stallings' attitudes began to shift from a self-centered bitterness to an other-related concern as he continued to search for answers to the absurdities of life, and, therefore, to move toward objectivity about war.

It was natural for Stallings to return to those earliest attractions which led to his participation in and condemnation of war since he continued to idealize the heroic man of action. Here was a code he could understand. Thus war, as Stallings saw it, became the supreme irony of his life. Mutilation and destruction resulting from the war destroyed romantic myths. Traumatic response led to the fictional "chronicle" which re-examined and re-created myth. But with myth's grasp came a reconciliation to reality and eventually the creation of the realistic interpretive chronicle. At the same time, he seemed to sense that man could not live without his myths. So between science and superstition, like any good humanist, he chose the latter. Suffering distilled the art, but through the art came relief and final reconciliation to the enigmatic man-artist.

Stallings' life and work appear to come full circle with the enthusiasm and patriotism of *The Doughboys*, both of which are presented as forcefully as the disillusionment and pacifism of *Plumes*. Unity is, of course, achieved in the body of his works by his making war the predominant theme. Whether he treated war in the novel, drama, the short story, a newspaper column, a film scenario, an essay or chronicle, there are recurring game motifs, images of romance, literary allusions (especially to Shakespeare), and repetitive phrases — all of which give additional unity to the corpus of his work. After *Plumes*, Stallings usually maintained one dominant attitude toward the fighting men, an attitude often reflected in the tone but explicit in the statement that, "Whatever may have been their faults, there was not a coward among them." We recall that he actually used the same statement in *Plumes* as well as in the 1959 essay, "The War to End War." And, while he hated and was fascinated by war, he could transcend it by understanding man in the midst of war — the most intensified form of life he had discovered.

A man who seems to have suffered from guilt, related perhaps to a feeling of inadequacy, Stallings suffered both physically and mentally as he sought recognition and approval in games of chance, games which dated back to his childhood days when he raced trains across a railroad trestle. His self-punishment actually resulted in a denial of his past — history, war, fiction, family, and property — or what one might consider his "first life" as a man of action who became disillusioned. But acceptance of and reconciliation to life resulted in his transcendence of the war, transcendence brought about with a happier "second life," as it were, through understanding some of its absurdities.

As a writer, he seems to have believed that he transcended fiction. His increasing concern for truth is reflected in his choice of scientific works, which constituted the main bulk of his reading in later years. But his Realistic chronicle *The Doughboys* was, perhaps, written more in recompense for those who, slighted by historians, were worthy of recognition — including himself. For Stallings, the memory of his actions was more important to him than thoughts reflected in his fiction. Thus he remained — to borrow Kenneth Burke's term — the "egoistic-altruistic" who devoted and sacrificed himself to that which sustained and protected him; and he did so in a work which embodies, artistically, his many versatile styles.

Stallings' personal paths of glory were as varied as the genres in which he wrote. Each of them, however, was related to competition. Ironically, Stallings' versatility as well as his transcendence of war and reconciliation with life very likely combined to deny readers any great bulk of fiction. And, unfortunately, the literati seem to include quantity as a requisite for consideration of quality. While Stallings' uncollected nonfiction would form several volumes of prose, the fact that his fiction is now so little known means that, despite his artistic ability in several forms, Stallings remains, for the most part, excluded from the study of American literature.

Not nearly so loyal in our literary tastes as Stallings was to his subject, we have failed to give him even minor author status. But, when I think of this author in relation to literary critics, I am reminded of a quotation from Nathaniel Hawthorne's *The Scarlet Letter:* "Sagaciously, under their spectacles, did they peep in the holds of vessels! Mighty was their fuss about little matters, and marvelous, sometimes, the obtuseness that allowed greater ones to slip between their fingers!"

We cannot read Stallings' works without our feeling that we have touched the man; for Laurence Stallings was Richard Plume, Hugh Dozier, Captain Flagg, the lieutenant in the big parade, the Marine in the hospital cheering for his corps, the chuckling witness to such outrageous incidents as those in "Turn Out the Guard." He was even the young boy impressed by the "moon-man's" uniform and by the brilliant cockade hat in "Gentleman in Blue." Finally, he was the chronicler who celebrated, in a way that no historian had captured, the heroic deeds of his comrades, among whom he wandered with an "Idaho willow leg." The interrelation of his life and work helps us to understand each more fully than we otherwise could, for they are, of course, inseparable.

Certainly, he was an exceptional man-artist and, perhaps, even *the* exceptional American author on war. His realistic picture of war teaches us much about patriotic as well as pacifist views and the resulting conflicts within. His personal life was that of a tragic hero who in the end, though legless, could lie in bed with a hat "cocked on the side of his head" and play another game, tell tales, laugh, and entertain his friends. Yet, I wonder if the joy he brought to others cheered him as much as it did them, or if his laughter and madcap antics shortly before his death were just another game — even if it was a game of life and played by a champion.

Notes and References

Preface

1. *Bookman*, LXII (May, 1926), 261.
2. "Lines for an Interment," *The New Republic*, LXXVI (September 20, 1933), 159.

Chapter One

1. Personal interview with Arthur Krock in Washington, D.C., February 10, 1971.
2. Letter from Frank E. Vandiver to me dated July 27, 1970, and post-marked Houston, Texas.
3. Telephone interview with Stallings' sister, Mrs. Preston Witherspoon, June 19, 1970.
4. Personal interview with Roland Neel in Macon, Georgia, June 17, 1970. Champney Holmes became an Atlanta surgeon but committed suicide.
5. *Plumes* (New York, 1924), p. 3.
6. Quoted by Sylvia Cheek, "Three Alumni Writers," *The Student, Wake Forest College*, LXX (November, 1959), 8-9.
7. Ibid., p. 8.
8. Specific dates for Stallings' military career were furnished by the Department of the Navy, Headquarters United States Marine Corps, Washington, D.C., through Senator Marlow W. Cook, July 2, 1970.
9. *The Doughboys* (New York, 1963), p. 106.
10. Personal interview with Roland Neel in Macon, Georgia, June 17, 1970.
11. Telephone interview with Helen Poteat Marshall, Boston, Massachusetts, June 3, 1970.
12. Margaret Case Harriman, *The Vicious Circle, The Story of the Algonquin Round Table* (New York, 1951), p. 11.
13. Ibid., p. 39.
14. Ibid., p. 78.
15. King Vidor, *A Tree Is a Tree* (New York, 1952), p. 171.

16. Ibid., p. 113.
17. Ibid., p. 112.
18. Ibid., p. 113.
19. Personal interview with Helen Poteat Marshall in Barnstable, Massachusetts, June 11, 1972.
20. Telephone interview with Mrs. Laurence Stallings, May 17, 1970.
21. "Celluloid Psychology," *The New Republic*, XXXIII (February 7, 1923), 282-83.
22. Letter from Robert Lovett to me dated February 10, 1971.
23. Ibid.
24. Letter to Arthur Krock, postmarked Whittier, California, March 2, 1962.
25. Letter to Arthur Krock, postmarked Whittier, California, February 1, 1963.
26. Stallings includes one paragraph about the later careers of some of his fighting friends (such as Merian C. Cooper, later a film producer and brigadier general in World War II) in *The Doughboys*, p. 255.
27. *The Best Plays of 1944-45*, ed. by Burns Mantle (New York, 1945), p. 7.
28. Telephone interview with Mrs. Laurence Stallings, May 17, 1970.
29. Stallings' description; letter to Arthur Krock, postmarked Los Angeles, July 26, 1964.
30. Letter from King Vidor to me dated May, 1970.
31. Personal interview with Mr. and Mrs. Roland Neel in Macon, Georgia, June 17, 1970.
32. Letter to me from Paul Green, postmarked Chapel Hill, North Carolina, February 19, 1971.
33. Letter to me from Lowell Thomas, postmarked Pawling, New York, February 1, 1971.
34. Letter to me from James M. Cain, postmarked Hyattsville, Maryland, February 12, 1971.
35. Ibid.
36. Letter to me from King Vidor, postmarked Beverly Hills, California, January 23, 1970.
37. *Letters of Sherwood Anderson*, ed. by Howard Mumford Jones, (Boston, 1953), pp. 148, 149, 253, 262, 304.
38. Letter from Laurence Stallings to Professor H. Edward Richardson, postmarked Whittier, California, June 28, 1960.
39. Telephone interview with Mrs. Preston Witherspoon, June 19, 1970.
40. "Laurence Stallings Dead at 73; 'What Price Glory?' Co-Author," *New York Times*, February 29, 1970, p. 37.

Chapter Two

1. *Plumes*. (New York: Harcourt Brace, 1924), p. 3.
2. Ibid., p. 4.

3. Ibid., p. 6.
4. Ibid., p. 7.
5. Ibid.
6. Ibid., p. 9.
7. Ibid., p. 10.
8. Ibid., p. 11.
9. Ibid., p. 13.
10. Ibid.
11. Ibid., p. 14.
12. Ibid., p. 15.
13. Ibid., p. 21.
14. Ibid., pp. 21-22.
15. Ibid., p. 19.
16. Ibid., p. 24.
17. John Harvey, *The Plantagenets* (New York, 1959), describes Richard Coeur de Lion (King Richard I of England) as the twelfth-century Crusader, who, in 1187, "took up the Cross" the day after news arrived of the defeat "of the Christians by Saladin" (p. 61). He describes him as "completely romantic in his devotion . . . utterly possessed by an ideal . . ." which was the "turning point in his life" (p. 61). This handsome, red-haired knight was nicknamed *Oc e No*, or "yea-and-Nay": "This has been represented as meaning that he blew hot and cold and never knew his own mind; but exactly the opposite was its intention. He was famous for the fact that whatever he said, that he did, never breaking the word he gave" (p. 50).
18. *Plumes*, p. 25.
19. Ibid., p. 32.
20. Dr. Dozier's prototype was Dr. William Louis Poteat, Stallings' biology professor; and Dr. Bibb was Dr. Hubert Poteat, Latin professor. In *Plumes*, however, Stallings has exchanged their disciplines. In the novel, "Bibbism" is what Stallings once described as "Poteatism": Writing of attending Wake Forest in 1912 ". . . when few Fundamentalists held Charles Darwin responsible for all the reproachful intelligence since the Renaissance," Stallings said that, "such a four-century growth, particularly among Baptists . . . was located and isolated at Wake Forest College. A great many of the faithful lumped all scientific intelligence under the opprobrious pseudonym of "Poteatism" ("Can a Man Be a Christian Today?," New York *World*, September 25, 1925, p. 13). In the novel *Plumes* Stallings describes "Bibbism" in this way: "Bibbism embraced the Bloody History of the Jews — known locally as the Word of God — in the midst of a world of many literatures and even more microscopes. . . . Thus young men who had dismissed the mystery of a universe by repeating after their lady Sunday-school teachers that 'God made the world in six days,' found their sixth day faith shaken by Dr. Bibb's freshman lectures on 'Bibbism' " (pp. 37-38).
21. *Plumes*, p. 45.
22. Ibid., p. 41.

23. Ibid., p. 24.

24. Ibid., p. 46.

25. This was the theme of Willa Cather's Pulitzer Prize-winning novel *One of Ours* (1923), which Stallings described as her favorite in a review of her literary career. But Stallings, in 1960, at Fullerton Junior College, Fullerton, California, said of *One of Ours* in an interview recorded by Professor Richardson: "She didn't tell the truth. That's what caused me to write *Plumes*."

26. *Plumes*, p. 46.

27. Ibid., p. 50. This, the third chapter, opens with an epigraph which might be interpreted literally since Plume, while at college, has not quite decided what he will be: "Opens his Plutarch, reads, dreams/Thus should I fight, save, or rule the world."

28. Ibid., p. 54.

29. Most of this chapter was later published as a short story, "Lt. Richard Plume Comes Home From the War," *Scholastic*, XXV (November 10, 1934), 4-6.

30. *Plumes*, p. 61.

31. Ibid., p. 66. In sharp contrast to the smell of ether among the wounded is the perfume of Esme. The scene is foreshadowed in the epigraph from Alfred Lord Tennyson's "Sir Galahad," 1842, 11. 9-12: "They reel, they roll, in clanging lists/And when the tide of combat stands/Perfume and flowers fall in showers/That lightly rain from ladies' hands."

32. Ibid., p. 67.

33. Ibid., p. 79.

34. Ibid., p. 90.

35. Ibid., p. 108.

36. Ibid., p. 112.

37. The book, published in 1883, is by the English naturalist essayist, and novelist, Richard Jefferies. It is in the library at "Forest Home."

38. *Plumes*, p. 118.

39. Ibid., p. 127.

40. Ibid., p. 128.

41. Ibid., p. 129.

42. Ibid.

43. Ibid., p. 164.

44. Ibid., p. 171. The first half of this quotation is quoted by V. L. Parrington in *Main Currents of American Thought* (New York, 1927) as the theme of *Plumes*, which he described as "a naturalistic novel" (p. 385).

45. Ibid., p. 189.

46. Ibid., p. 193.

47. Ibid., p. 196.

48. Ibid., p. 195.

49. Ibid., p. 198.

50. Ibid., pp. 198-99.

51. Ibid., p. 202.
52. Ibid., p. 204.
53. Ibid., p. 216.
54. Ibid., p. 221.
55. Ibid., p. 239.
56. Ibid., pp. 243-44.
57. Ibid., pp. 247-48.
58. Ibid., p. 257.
59. Chapter 11, the first chapter in Book Four, opens with an epigraph from Thomas Campbell's battle poem "Hohenlinden" (1802): "The combat deepens, Oh, ye brave/Who rush to glory or the grave."
60. *Plumes*, p. 269.
61. Ibid., p. 318.
62. Ibid., p. 311.
63. Appropriately, Chapter 13 opens with an epigraph taken from Tennyson's "Sir Galahad": "My good sword carveth the casques of men/My tough lance thrusteth sure/My strength is as the strength of ten/Because my heart is pure."
64. The epigraph for the final chapter is taken from Thomas B. Macaulay's "The Battle of Naseby" (1824): "Press where ye see my white plume shine/Amidst the ranks of war." The lines serve to define the content which follows in Chapter 14 — and also as the novel's opening epigraph for the title page. Stallings' use of lines from Macaulay's works is especially relevant in that all of them stress the historical background. Considered by some as very influential in determining the nineteenth-century concept of history, Macaulay "distrusted deductive reasoning," detested radicals, and "called for compromise rather than Revolution" (*The Victorian Age*, edited with introductions by John Wilson Bowyer and John Lee Brooks, [New York, 1954], p. 26).
65. *Plumes*, p. 325.
66. Ibid., p. 326.
67. Ibid., pp. 337-38.
68. Ibid., p. 345.
69. Ibid., p. 161.
70. Ibid., pp. 249-50.
71. Ibid., p. 82.
72. Ibid., p. 99.
73. Ibid., p. 50.
74. Ibid., p. 80.

Chapter Three

1. Stallings and Anderson reviewed the writing history of their play in November, 1924, for *Current Opinion* ("How a Great Play is Written," LXXVII, 617). Stallings felt that the "Marines could provide good stage

material" for a musical; Anderson, "that there was dramatic material way beyond the requirements of musical comedy. . . ." Anderson "appeared one day with a rough manuscript" which included a second act that was "vague and colorless." Stallings took the manuscript and began to rewrite it: "The dugout in his hands, began to resemble a real dugout and the people emerged as startling true counterfeits of the frightened and brave and lofty and shallow and stalwart and maimed boys and men who really lived in it."

2. *Literary History of the United States*, ed. by Robert E. Spiller (New York, 1949), II, 1317.

3. *Three American Plays* (New York, 1926), p. 1. All quotations from the three plays, *What Price Glory?*, *First Flight*, and *The Buccaneer* are taken from this edition.

4. Similar to the buffoonery of Flagg and Quirt is that of returning Marines described in Stallings' "A Christmas Story," New York *World*, December 25, 1925, p. 17, where Stallings wrote about the Marines' outwitting the Army in getting off ship in order to rush to a bar.

5. "The War to End War," *American Heritage*, X (October, 1959), 84.

6. *Three American Plays*, p. 21.

7. Ibid., p. 66.

8. Ibid., p. 71.

9. Ibid., p. 54.

10. Ibid., p. 55.

11. Ibid.

12. *Plumes*, p. 326.

13. *Three American Plays*, pp. 59-60.

14. *Plumes*, p. 243.

15. *Three American Plays*, p. 60.

16. Ibid., p. 73.

17. Ibid., p. 42.

18. A friend for forty years, retired Army Air Force General Merian C. Cooper said: "The theme of Stallings' famous play . . . was that courageous men don't talk about glory, nor do they talk about honor. They only die for those things" (Quoted in obituary, "Macon Playwright L. Stallings Dies," Atlanta *Journal*, February 29, 1968).

19. *The Best Plays of 1924-25* (New York, 1925), pp. 30-31. Laurence Stallings' name appears first as co-author with Anderson in this work as it also appears under the 1924 copyright listing.

20. Joseph Wood Krutch, *The American Drama Since 1918* (New York, 1939), p. 39. Krutch reflected the concern of others with the language of the play, and he included an interesting anecdote about its powerful infectiousness: ". . . a gentle grandmother, who was observed searching the floor after the performance, replied to a query from the young man who had brought her to the performance by remarking with absentminded mildness, 'I've lost my god-dam spectacles' " (p. 35).

21. Arthur Hobson Quinn, *A History of the American Drama From the Civil War to the Present Day* (New York, 1927), pp. 234-235.

22. The great success of the stage play, then as now, led it to Hollywood; and, in 1926, the film was released by Twentieth Century Fox. Directed by Raoul Walsh, the movie differed from the play. For one thing the language had to be cleaned up for movie-goers, a fact which provoked one critic in "Strange Screen Confidences" (*Literary Digest*, XCII [March 5, 1927], 24) to write about his efforts to read lips since this was the "manner in which cursing was received." The reviewer described the movie as a mixture of "blasphemy, obscenity, vulgarity and violence — everything, in fact, that could shock the feeling of a nation which knew war as an excuse for triumphal parades and marches."

Hardly shocking today, *What Price Glory?* was remade and re-released in 1957. An additional romance was added for a young Marine (Lewisohn). Throughout the movie, the camera constantly focused on the face of the frightened soldier Moore who asked, *"What Price Glory?"*

Malcolm Cowley in "Lines for an Interment" (*The New Republic*, LXXV [September 20, 1933], p. 160) has commented on the ironic fate of the original play: "People at first regarded it as pacifist propaganda, but pretty soon the movies got hold of it, and the publicity department of the United States Marine Corps got hold of it, reduced it to its essence, stirred in a few brass bands and bistros — and the result was those gay devil-dogs, Captain Flagg and Sergeant Quirt, urging young men by their heroic example to join the Marines and sleep with foreign women." But that publicity was for a later generation and another war.

23. Harlan Hatcher, *Creating the Modern American Novel* (New York, 1935), p. 226.

24. Krutch, in *The American Drama Since 1918*, p. 54, wrote of the authors' failure to match the success of *What Price Glory?*: ". . . the similarity between the earliest play and the two last is confined to superficialities in tone and method. All have a certain romantic dash and a hearty air of robustious delight in daring adventure, but only the first touches any complex of vivid contemporary emotions. Neither the story of Andrew Jackson's youth told in *First Flight* nor the story of Pirate Morgan told in *The Buccaneer* becomes more than cloak and sword [sic] melodrama. *What Price Glory?* had romantic dash and robustious adventurousness. But it happened also to deal with incidents which the audience itself was ready to clothe with emotion."

In a review for *Nation*, CXXI (October 7, 1925), 390-91, Krutch called *First Flight* "the first native historical drama which is neither merely a stately tableau nor a mildly galvanized war-works."

25. Stallings used this phrase in regard to William Faulkner and *Sartoris* in a letter to Professor H. Edward Richardson dated June 28, 1960, from Whittier, California.

26. In *Plumes,* p. 10; Charity was one of Christian Plume's four children, who inherited nothing from Christian.

27. In "The Whole Art of a Wooden Leg," *The Smart Set,* LXX (March, 1923), 107-11, Stallings opens his essay with the quotation "He jests at scars, who never felt a wound" but he treats, with humor, some of the lessons in mobility which he has learned.

28. In 1944, Stallings wrote another play, *The Streets Are Guarded,* which was never published (and is unavailable) but which was produced by John C. Wilson. A synopsis of the play, which ran for only twenty-four performances, is included in *Best Plays of 1944-45,* ed. by Burns Mantle (New York, 1945), p. 398: "The Marine escapes Bataan and makes his way in an open boat several hundred miles southward. Landing on a small island, he finds two airmen, three Navy men, and a Dutch nurse. Tom Jelks, pharmacist's mate, delirious with fever, has prayed for a miracle. Let the Lord send quinine and a savior. He accepts the Marine as an answer to his prayer. The others are sufficiently affected to insist that the Marine, who is wearing his dead Captain's helmet, shall become their leader. With Memphis Jones's help, the Marine invades a neighboring island and steals medicines and a walkie-talkie radio from the Japs. With the medicines the pharmacist's mate is cured; with the radio help is summoned. The Marine disappears. Miracle or not? Who knows?"

Chapter Four

1. *Plumes,* p. 243.

2. Ibid., p. 208.

3. "The Big Parade," *The New Republic,* XL (September 17, 1924), 66.

4. Ibid.

5. Ibid. Stallings' repetitious use of "seven" in relation to hell begins in *Plumes* where both Noah and Richard suffer seven burning wounds.

6. "The Big Parade," p. 68.

7. King Vidor, in *A Tree Is a Tree,* spoke of the movie version of "The Big Parade," calling "the march through Belleau Wood" the scene that "gripped the viewing audience." Vidor used "A.E.F. veterans who had served time in France" and instructed the men that each step had to be taken on a drumbeat, "each turn of the head, lift of a rifle, pull of a trigger. . . ." He added that the veterans thought he "had gone completely daft" and that one British veteran wanted to know if they "were performing in some bloody ballet. I did not say so at the time, but that is exactly what it was — a bloody ballet, a ballet of death" (p. 116).

8. In "Enlisted Men Only," New York *World,* November 26, 1924, Stallings reviews some doughboy sketches by Leonard H. Nason, a "member of the A.E.F.," and quotes the following passage from Nason's story "The Casual's Return": "In hospital those birds come over at night and lay great big eggs the size of a steam boiler around. The night I was in the evacuation hospital at Coulommiers . . . one dropped three of them on

us. It blew the Y.M.C.A. tent and tent next to the one I was in all to hell and it was night too; no machine guns to drive him away. Just lie there in your pajamas and wait to be bumped off. . . . There was a cross on our front lawn too." Stallings adds that he "was in that tent," the setting for "Esprit de Corps."

9. "Esprit de Corps," *Scribner's*, LXXXIV (August, 1928), 212.

10. Ibid.

11. Ibid., p. 213.

12. Ibid., p. 224.

13. Ibid.

14. Ibid.

15. In *The Doughboys*, pp. 112-13, Stallings gives this real account: "The first messenger bearing tidings from Vaux to the marines in one tent was a giant Doughboy captain, legs now in splints, overseas cap with the infantry's blue cord for piping still on his head. He sat erect on his stretcher, drunk on ether fumes, shouting happily as orderlies lurched down aisles of grass toward the row of beds prepared at high speed by Army nurses from Council Bluffs, Iowa. 'Oh, the goddam sonsabitches,' the captain shouted joyously. 'The headline-hunting bastards! We showed the sonsabitches how to do it!' No one in that tent thought the captain's remarks applied to the sonsabitches in Colonel General von Boehn's German Seventh Army. . . . By noon, awaking thick-mouthed to gag down his tin plateful of an eye-stinging salmon salad . . . the Doughboy captain was courtesy itself to the Leatherneck runner of Italian origin minus a leg in the neighboring bed."

16. "WAR: Capt. Stallings Heads Fox-NANA Ethiopian Expedition," *Newsweek*, VI (August 17, 1935), 31.

17. *Plumes*, p. 79.

18. Ibid., p. 139.

19. "Turn Out the Guard," *Saturday Evening Post*, October 13, 1928, 16.

20. Ibid., p. 92.

21. Ibid., p. 16.

22. Ibid. In *Plumes* (p. 24), Stallings referred to Zachary as a "Bayard of a Southern town," but he first used the term "Bayardist" in relation to Robert E. Lee, "Lee and Jackson," New York *World*, May 11, 1925, p. 13. He defined the term as one who fights alongside his men.

23. "Turn Out the Guard," p. 97.

24. Ibid., p. 98.

25. Ibid.

26. Major James G. Harbord of the U.S. Cavalry is one such character. In *The Doughboys*, Stallings describes Harbord's being summoned "to Chaumont on July 26 after his division was relieved from the fighting in the Second Battle of the Marne" (p. 172). Harbord expected "command of a corps" but was ordered "to command the Service of Supply." Stallings describes him as a leader who "pleaded for any sort of emolument; a button or an emblem he might bestow. . . ." (p. 176). Another character is Hunter

Liggett "later lieutenant general and commander of the American First Army on the Meuse" who took up horseback riding in order to "reduce his corporation" (p. 154). Stallings tells of his taking a "bone-shaking fall" but getting back on his horse "before anyone could dismount to attend him." Stallings concludes this episode with: "This agility — some fat men are extraordinarily graceful — was reported to Chaumont, and Liggett was given a corps" (p. 154).

27. *Plumes*, p. 305.

28. "Turn Out the Guard," p. 98.

29. *Plumes*, p. 46.

30. "Vale of Tears," *Cosmopolitan*, XC (May, 1931), 26-30ff. My source of reference is *Men at War*, edited and introduced by Ernest Hemingway (New York, 1942), p. 377. The Marine outfit is the same as Stallings'.

31. In *Plumes*, a wounded veteran, Lieutenant Jackson (who is a mulatto) lies in the bed next to Richard Plume while Plume recuperates from the fall on ice. Plume admires Jackson's art work, and Jackson teaches Plume his craft (p. 266).

32. "Vale of Tears," p. 382.

33. Ibid., p. 386.

34. Ibid., p. 388.

35. Ibid., pp. 395-96.

36. Nurse Adair is probably patterned after "Miss Laconuis," described in the Epilogue of *The Doughboys* as the one "with whom I had fallen in love — along with fifty-one others" (p. 372).

37. "Vale of Tears," p. 403.

38. Ibid., p. 404.

39. Ibid.

40. Ibid., p. 406.

41. Ibid., p. 409.

42. Letter from Laurence Stallings to Professor H. Edward Richardson, postmarked Whittier, California, dated June 28, 1960.

43. Ibid.

44. *Plumes*, p. 102.

45. Telephone interview with Stallings' daughter, Sally, Fresno, California, February 7, 1970. (Stallings refers to the battle of Yellow Tavern in *Plumes*, p. 87.) "Gentleman in Blue" was later anthologized, unchanged, as "Near Appomattox," in *The Fighting American*, ed. by Vernon Mason (New York, 1943).

46. "Gentleman in Blue," *Saturday Evening Post*, (February 20, 1932), 9.

47. Ibid.

48. Ibid., p. 95.

49. Ibid., p. 9.

50. Ibid., p. 8.

51. Ibid., p. 95.

52. Ibid.

53. Ibid.
54. Ibid., p. 9.
55. Ibid., p. 95.
56. *Plumes*, p. 32.
57. Ibid., p. 129.
58. "Gentleman in Blue" (1932) bears a marked resemblance to William Faulkner's later story "Ambuscade," *Saturday Evening Post*, (September 29, 1934), pp. 12-13, and Stallings' story may have been a source for Faulkner. "Ambuscade" became the first chapter of Faulkner's *The Unvanquished* (New York, 1938).

Faulkner's story is also recalled in the first person by the twelve-year-old Bayard, who, with friend Ringo, sees a Yankee soldier ride toward his house. He thinks, "He looks just like a man" (p. 28). He and Ringo get a musket from the house and return to their hiding place; when Bayard twice asks Ringo, "Do you want to be free?," Ringo shouts, "Shoot the bastud" (p. 31); and Bayard kills the horse but thinks he killed the man. Other Yankee troops arrive to search the house but to no avail. The family, having buried its silverware and other valuables, watches as the search takes place. The Yankee colonel is quite aware that the two boys are hiding under their Granny's skirts, but he courteously acknowledges Granny, lies, and dismisses his men. Granny then offers the colonel a "glass of cool milk" (p. 37). Of the officer's departure, Faulkner writes, ". . . Louvinia said he was standing there in the door, with brass bright on his dark blue and his hat in his hand . . . looking at Granny without laughing now: 'I won't apologize; fools cry out at wind or fire. But permit me to say and hope that you will never have anything worse than this to remember us by' " (p. 38).

59. "Return to the Woods," *Collier's* (March 5, 1932), 30.
60. Ibid.
61. Ibid., p. 31. The same episode is included, only slightly changed, in *The Doughboys*, pp. 96-97, as follows:

The orchard was small and plain, and much as the captain had imagined it, apple trees above a fine stone wall six feet high with a broken-glass crown to thwart any urchin who did not have a corduroy jacket thick enough to pad the jagged teeth. Someone had replaced the gate on its iron strap hinges, the gate he had removed from speedier access to Chauchats, Hotchkisses, and a captured Maxim placed there to repel the many probings in the dark. The two friends pulled the bell rope and a young woman appeared, auburn-haired, pale from a recent confinement, a pallid baby blinking at her breast. The two friends explained that they had done some fighting around the orchard and would like to sit there for time to smoke a cigarette. "Then it was you who defiled our orchard," said the young Frenchwoman, narrowing the distance between gate and gatepost. . . . "You did not save my village, M'sieu," the young mother went on. "You ruined the soil of the orchard. Every year we dig up the empty *cartouches* from *les mitrailleuses*. The brass can be tasted in the fruit itself, M'sieu. When you left, why did you not clean up our orchard? Take your sordid *cartouches* with you?" She closed the gate without haste.

62. "Return to the Woods," p. 52.
63. Ibid., p. 31.
64. Ibid.
65. Ibid.
66. Ibid., p. 52.
67. Ibid.
68. Ibid.
69. Ibid.
70. Stallings' actual return to those woods on June 6, 1925 — the anniversary of the first day of battle at Belleau Wood — is related in Chapter 6 of *The Doughboys.*
71. Plumes, p. 197.
72. Ibid., p. 188
73. Ibid., 170.
74. In *The Doughboys,* pp. 123-24, Stallings gives a similar account of "Corporal Alvey C. Martz from Pennsylvania's lonely Somerset County, who was stringing barbed wire on the river bank with a patrol of six men when Bruchmuller's guns opened." Alvey belonged to "C Company", and Stallings adds: "(Why this lad, who had never been to war, who had never undergone a patrol exercise in a quiet sector, should have been placed there at the known zero hour is something that Degoutte, who all along had wanted the Yanks to fight this way, could never explain to Pershing). Martz and his six buddies dropped into shell holes."
75. "The War to End War," p. 85.

Chapter Five

1. "Arnold Bennett's Journal, Vol. 2, and Marvelous — It Covers the War Period," New York *Sun,* November 15, 1932, p. 24.
2. Arnold Bennett — along with H. G. Wells and H. L. Mencken — is named by Margaret Case Harriman in *The Vicious Circle* as one of its members' "gods," who were often invited to the Round Table as guests and welcomed "with respectful, though not slavish attention" (p. 208).
Stallings helped promote *American Mercury,* begun by H. L. Mencken and George J. Nathan, in these articles: "A New Magazine," New York *World,* December 24, 1923, p. 7; "A Literary Journey," *World,* January 20, 1924, p. 6; "A Critical Journey," *World,* January 30, 1924, p. 9; "April Magazines," *World,* March 28, 1924, p. 13. He also wrote articles about Mencken and his work: "American as She Is Wrote in Several of These States," New York *World,* October 18, 1925, p. 6; "The Cream of the Scrapings," *World,* July 25, 1925, p. 7; and he devoted two columns to a review of Isaac Goldberg's *The Man Mencken:* "Mencken of the Sun," *World,* November 23, 1925, p. 11, and "More Mencken," *World,* November 25, 1925, p. 13.
3. "Arnold Bennett's Journal, Vol. 2, and Marvelous . . . ," p. 24.

4. "Relic of the Doughboy Newspaper Embalmed for Our Derision," New York *Sun*, September 18, 1931, p. 52.

5. Ibid.

6. Stallings' favorite, *Through the Wheat* by Thomas Boyd, received fewer lines than did his least favorite, Willa Cather's *One of Ours*. In a long article commemorating her "being awarded a doctorate in letters at Princeton," Stallings reviewed her entire literary career; but his main purpose seemed to be to justify his own opinion (he felt that she "didn't tell the truth"), a purpose stated in the title to his article, "Miss Cather's Favorite Among Her Novels Is Ignored in Her Princeton Citation," New York *Sun*, June 18, 1932, p. 29.

He panned John Dos Passos' *Three Soldiers* in "Mr. Dos Passos in Muft [*sic*]," New York *World*, November 14, 1923, p. 13; but he especially liked Henri Barbusse's *Under Fire*, which he mentions in a review of Barbusse's *Chains* ("Fiction and Fact," New York *World*, November 2, 1925, p. 13).

7. Stallings describes the pieces as "memories of the action at Soissons and Blanc Mont." Stallings' article is primarily aimed at promoting the works of Thomason; he suggests what should be published and where as he praises Thomason's writing and drawing.

8. "One of Ours," New York *World*, September 23, 1925, p. 11.

9. Ibid.

10. "Richard's Himself Again," New York *World*, March 30, 1925, p. 13.

11. "Well, You Heard It Before," New York *World*, August 17, 1925, p. 11. This review is interesting for the biographical information included. Three-fourths of the article deals with the summer spent in Europe though Stallings does not mention his return to Belleau Wood. He comes home with a greater appreciation for the foreign literary masters — Flaubert, Balzac — only to lament the increasing number of "inconsequential and trivial novels" coming from the presses. He refers to all "the racket over Theodore Dreiser" that had been taking place during the summer: "The literary magazines are filled with Dreiser. Mr. Mencken backs him, with Lewis, against the English-writing world. Yet Dreiser, for me, always will remain a lesser Zola, exceedingly dull for the most part, and not possessed of even the occasional afflatus of that Frenchman."

12. "Enlisted Men Only," New York *World*, November 26, 1924, p. 13.

13. "The Education of Dr. Kerkhoven & Co.," New York *Sun*, January 27, 1932, p. 25.

14. Ibid.

15. "Aesthete, 1879 Model," New York *World*, September 21, 1925, p. 13.

16. Ibid.

17. "Drunk with Sacrifice," New York *World*, May 12, 1924, p. 11.

18. Ibid.

19. Ibid.

20. *Plumes*, p. 243.

21. Ibid, pp. 215-216.

22. "Lee and Jackson," New York *World*, May 11, 1925, p. 13.

23. Ibid.

24. Ibid.

25. Ibid.

26. Ibid.

27. *The First World War: A Pictorial History* (New York, 1933, 1962). The two editions have the same pagination for photographs. A second introduction is added to the 1962 edition.

28. Quoted on the dust jacket to the 1962 edition.

29. "The War to End War,"*American Heritage*, X (October, 1959), 6.

30. *The First World War*, p. 129.

31. Ibid., p. 204.

32. Ibid., p. 283.

33. Ibid., p. 284.

34. Ibid., p. 240.

35. Ibid., p. 97.

36. Ibid., p. 98.

37. Ibid., pp. 285-86.

38. Ibid., pp. 287-88.

39. "Lest We Forget," *Saturday Review*, X (August 5, 1933), 25-27. General March, Chief of Staff of the U.S. Army at the end of the war, praised its "stark realism." Jane Addams thought the book was "wonderfully well done both in technique and the selection of photographs" (p. 25).She put the book on display in "the booth at the International Congress of Women in Chicago."

The editor and publishers were praised by Villard for "so moving and so truthful a volume," but Major General O'Ryan called it "no work of art," adding, however, "that circumstance, rather adds to its acceptability" (p. 25). Frederic Palmer appreciated the work and its editor, and Thomas Boyd wrote that the book deepens "the realization that it will take more than peace conferences to dispel the threat in the title" (p. 26). Boyd describes Stallings' arrangement as "excellent."

Hervey Allen's comments were the most enthusiastic:

All that can be done with the visual sense to give the reader . . . a personal experience of warfare has been accomplished. The photograph editing is superb and Mr. Stallings' captions little less than miraculous. Only the stench and the nerve shattering sounds that accompany war are lacking to bring about a complete vicarious recall of the first World War. To me these pages prove conclusively that the economic theory of history is the bunk; that nationalism was, and continues to be, a potent religion for which men are willing to commit suicide en masse, and that those who think that the affairs of this man-infested planet are to be settled by woolly doctors of logic on a junket to Geneva are sick in the head. (p. 27)

40. Ibid., p. 26.

41. The success of *The First World War* led to the filming in 1934 by the Fox Film Corporation, for which Stallings was editor-in-chief. Stallings

wrote the dialogue for the film which was dedicated "to the soldiers and sailors, known and unknown, who fought the Great War, and to the cameramen, known and unknown whose work made" the film possible. Like the book, the film began with the buildup for war; but it ended with the Armistice and with men of different nationalities crossing lines to shake hands and exchange cigarettes. With the final statement, "But today there is another generation," the last camera shot was of Germans and Americans exchanging hats.

42. "Lines for an Interment," *The New Republic*, LXXVI (September 20, 1933), 159-61.

43. Ibid., p. 160.

44. Ibid., p. 161.

45. "The Dead of the Next War," *The New Republic*, LXXVI (October 4, 1931), 214-16.

46. Ibid., p. 216.

47. "War, Response, and Contradiction," *The Philosophy of Literary Form* (Baton Rouge, Louisiana; 1941), pp. 236-37.

48. Ibid., p. 237.

49. Ibid., p. 256.

50. Harlan Hatcher, *Creating the Modern American Novel*, p. 227.

51. *Anon.*, "Stallings on Way to Cover the War," New York *Times*, August 8, 1935, p. 7.

52. During the years before and after his Ethiopian assignment, Stallings continued working on films, such as *Song of the West* (1930), *Billy the Kid* (1931), *Women of All Nations* (1931), *Big Executive Party* (1933), *After Office Hours* (1935), *So Red the Rose* (1935), and *Too Hot to Handle* (1938). During the 1940's he worked on these films: *Jungle Book* (1942), *Northwest Passage* (1940), *Salome Where She Danced* (1945), *Christmas Eve* (1947), *A Miracle Can Happen* (1948), and *She Wore a Yellow Ribbon* (1949). One of the few screen plays available to me was *Song of the West*, a film version of *Rainbow*, done with Oscar Hammerstein II, and produced in New York in 1928.

Song of the West is a story of "forty-niners" journeying to California to look for "the pot of gold at the end of the rainbow." The lead male, Stanton, is an ex-soldier who had fled a court martial after an officer maliciously reported Stanton's involvement in a fight. Disguised as a parson, Stanton joins the wagon train and falls in love with the Colonel's daughter, Virginia. Members of the regiment escorting the train recognize Stanton, who is described as a man who "couldn't stand being out of the army," a gentleman who misses "being in a blue coat." He has to leave the wagon train, but Virginia follows, and the two marry.

Unable to find any other employment, Stanton becomes a gambler; but a year later, when Virginia's friends appear at the saloon, Stanton is ashamed of the life they are living and of the effect it has had on his wife. Realizing that she belongs with "her own people," he deserts her and heads for

California alone. In the end, the two are reunited as Stanton is received by the Colonel — by then the military governor of California — and again is accepted into the army. Stanton says to a friend: "I've been in tighter places this year than I ever was in the army . . . but there was no brass . . . no blue . . . and no cut to the clothes. You feel so safe in a blue coat. She knows it . . . and she'll know tonight that inside of me I've been afraid ever since I lost mine." The story ends with Virginia's proudly commenting "You've got your blue coat back at last."

Stanton's fascination for the blue coat is reminiscent of the young boy's attraction in Stallings' story "Gentleman in Blue." But the themes of guilt and insecurity which in *Plumes* are related to Richard's hatred of himself for throwing his life away now reappear in a different context.

53. "Italians Confident of Speedy Victory," New York *Times*, August 21, 1935. p. 4

54. "Ethiopians Carry Trucks Across Streams," New York *Times*, September 17, 1935, p. 17.

55. Ibid.

56. In a long article "Bush Brigades and Blackamoors," *American Mercury*, XXXVII (April 1936), Stallings described numerous foreign heroes in the Ethiopian conflict.

57. "Ethiopians Count on British," New York *Times*, September 28, 1935. p. 14.

58. "Ethiopia Is Aghast at 'Civilized War,' " New York *Times*, October 14, 1935, p. 11

59. In his war dispatches from Ethiopia, Stallings does not comment on the personal danger to himself or to his crew. However, later that year, in a suit against the Fox Film Corporation by the International Flight Corporation, it was made evident. The plaintiff "applied in Supreme Court . . . to take the testimony of Laurence Stallings and other editors of Movietonews before trial . . . on the ground that the world-wide pursuit of newsreel shots may prevent Mr. Stallings and other witnesses from being on hand when the trial is held. Mr. Smith pointed out that Mr. Stallings risked his life covering the Italo-Ethiopian War and may at any time set off for some distant point" ("Stallings Bored by Own Play Now," New York *Times*, October 30, 1936, p. 25).

60. "The War to End War," *American Heritage*, X (October, 1959), 84.

61. "The War to End War," p. 85.

62. Ibid.

Chapter Six

1. *The Doughboys* (New York, 1963), pp. iii-iv.

2. Ibid., pp. 367-68.

3. Ibid., p. 1.

4. Ibid., p. 3.
5. Ibid., p. 6.
6. Ibid., p. 23.
7. Ibid., p. 37.
8. Ibid.
9. Ibid., p. 136.
10. Ibid., p. 134.
11. Ibid., p. 310.
12. Ibid., p. 315.
13. Ibid., p. 360.
14. Ibid., p. 2.
15. Ibid., p. 258.
16. Ibid., pp. 339-40.
17. Ibid., pp. 155-56.
18. Ibid., p. 215.
19. Ibid., p. 314.
20. Ibid., p. 287. A longer and more interesting treatment of World War I songs, "the finest outlet for the tenseness of discipline," is Stallings' article, "Songs My Mother Never Taught Me," *Collier's* (June 4, 1927), pp. 12-13, 41. In addition to verses originated on the march there are references to the alteration of tunes such as George M. Cohan's "Over There," which, according to Stallings, "was transmuted from the dull brass of a yawping patriotism to the pure gold of a soldier's fancy, and came out as Underwear, Underwear, Scratching Here, Scratching There, Everywhere . . ." (p. 13).
21. *The Doughboys*, pp. 323-28.
22. Ibid., p. 215.
23. Ibid., p. 217.
24. Equally interesting are accounts of Joyce Kilmer's death, or of Eddie Rickenbacker's favorite pilot, Lieutenant Sherry ("Madame Sherry," p. 216). And Stallings' annotated "A Reader's Guide" includes lengthy descriptions of every work he had read on World War I, along with personal opinions and such comments as this in relation to "other fronts": ". . . personally I lean to Ernest Hemingway's *A Farewell to Arms* . . . for a description of that Italian disaster" (p. 386).
25. *The Doughboys*, p. 67.
26. Ibid., p. 106.
27. Ibid., pp. 106-107.
28. Plume sought work at Green Crescent Drug Company but was rejected. He met unusually nasty people in the city: one "a rather gaseous and undersized fellow, in a green suit" (p. 101); a clerk named Mr. Green, who interviewed the Plumes for an apartment lease (p. 164); and a salesman who had suits which "all seemed infected with a greenish yarn" (p. 211). And in "Esprit de Corps" Stallings, describing the dying major surveying his wound, wrote: "One almost expected him to say to his adjutant: Mr.

Green, the enemy is making progress against the corotid artery. Please tell the 74th Company of white corpuscles to form line of skirmishers to the left and dig in. They must hold collarbone ridge at all costs" (p. 213).

29. *The Doughboys*, p. 373.

30. Ibid., p. 374.

31. Ibid., p. 205.

32. Ibid., p. 1.

33. Eldridge Colby, *Best Sellers*, XXIII (June 15, 1963), 111.

34. "They Were There, Lafayette," *Saturday Review*, XLVI (July 6, 1963), 28.

35. "What It's Like Over There," New York *Herald Tribune Books*, June 9, 1963, p. 5.

Selected Bibliography

PRIMARY SOURCES

"Aesthete, 1879 Model." New York *World*, September 21, 1925, p. 13.
"American as She Is Wrote in Several of These States." New York *World*, October 18, 1925, p. 6.
"April Magazines." New York *World*, March 28, 1924, p. 13.
"Arnold Bennett's Journal, Vol. 2, and Marvelous — It Covers the War Period." New York *Sun*, November 15, 1932, p. 24.
"The Big Parade." *The New Republic*, XL (September 17, 1924), 66-69.
"Bloody Belleau Wood." *American Heritage*, XLVC (June, 1963), 77.
"Bush Brigades and Blackamoors." *American Mercury*, XXXVII (April, 1936), 411-19.
"Can a Man Be a Christian Today?" New York *World*, September 25, 1925, p. 13.
"Celluloid Psychology." *The New Republic*, XXXIII (February 7, 1923), 282-83.
"A Christmas Story." New York *World*, December 25, 1925, p. 17.
"The Cream of the Scrapings." New York *World*, July 25, 1925, p. 7.
"A Critical Journey." New York *World*, January 30, 1924, p. 9.
The Doughboys. New York: Harper and Row, 1963.
"Drunk With Sacrifice." New York *World*, May 12, 1924, p. 11.
"The Education of Dr. Kerkhoven & Co." New York *Sun*, January 27, 1932, p. 25.
"Enlisted Men Only." New York *World*, November 26, 1924, p. 13.
"Esprit de Corps." *Scribner's*, LXXXIV (August, 1928), 212-15.
"Ethiopia Is Aghast at 'Civilized War.' " New York *Times*, October 14, 1935, p. 11.
"Ethiopians Carry Trucks Across Stream." New York *Times*, September 17, 1935, p. 4.
"Ethiopians Count on British." New York *Times*, September 28, 1935, p. 4.
"Fiction and Fact." New York *World*, November 2, 1925, p. 13.
The First World War: A Pictorial History. New York: Simon and Schuster, 1933, 1962.
"Gentleman in Blue." *Saturday Evening Post*, February 20, 1932, pp. 8-9.

"Great Scott." New York *World*, April 22, 1925, p. 13.
"How a Great Play Is Written." *Current Opinion*, LXXVII (November, 1924), 617.
"Lee and Jackson." New York *World*, May 11, 1925, p. 13.
Letter to Professor H. Edward Richardson, postmarked Whittier, California, June 28, 1960.
"A Literary Journey." New York *World*, January 20, 1924, p. 6.
"Lt. Richard Plume Comes Home From the War." *Scholastic*, XXV (November 10, 1934), 4-6.
"Mencken of the *Sun*." New York *World*, November 23, 1925, p. 11.
"Miss Cather's Favorite Among Her Novels Is Ignored in Her Princeton Citation." New York *Sun*, June 18, 1932, p. 29.
"More Mencken." New York *World*, November 25, 1925, p. 13.
"Mr. Dos Passos in Muft [*sic*]." New York *World*, November 14, 1923, p. 13.
"A New Magazine." New York *World*, December 24, 1923, p. 7.
"One of Ours." New York *World*, September 23, 1925, p. 11.
"Paths of Glory." New York *World*, February 8, 1924, p. 11.
Plumes. New York: Harcourt Brace, 1924.
"Relic of the Doughboy Newspaper Embalmed for Our Derision." New York *Sun*, September 18, 1931, p. 12.
"Return to the Woods." *Collier's*, March 5, 1932, pp. 30-31, 52.
"Richard's Himself Again." New York *World*, March 30, 1925, p. 13.
"The Simple Annals of a Disappointed General, A Clever Little People the Europeans." New York *Sun*, September 25, 1931, p. 5.
Song of the West. Metro-Goldwyn-Mayer, 1930.
"Some Prejudices." New York *World*, September 2, 1925, p. 11.
"Songs My Mother Never Taught Me." *Collier's*, June 4, 1927, pp. 12-13, 41.
Three American Plays [What Price Glory?, First Flight, and *The Buccaneer]*. New York: Harcourt Brace, 1926.
"Turn Out the Guard." *Saturday Evening Post*, October 13, 1928, pp. 16-17.
"Vale of Tears." *Men at War*. Edited and introduced by Ernest Hemingway. New York: Crown Publishing Company, 1942.
"The War to End War." *American Heritage*, X (October, 1959), 6-8, 84-85.
"Well You Heard It Before." New York *World*, August 17, 1925, p. 11.
"The Whole Art of a Wooden Leg." *The Smart Set*, LXX (March, 1923), 107-11.

SECONDARY SOURCES

BURKE, KENNETH. *The Philosophy of Literary Form*. Baton Rouge: Louisiana State University Press, 1941. Uses Stallings' *The First World War* as his point of departure in "War, Response and Contradiction."
CHEEK, SYLVIA. "Three Alumni Writers." *The Student, Wake Forest College*, LXX (November, 1959), 8-9. Interview in which Stallings reminisces about his college years.

COLBY, ELDRIDGE. *Best Sellers*, XXIII (June 15, 1963), 111. Reviews *The Doughboys;* calls chapter on Belleau Wood "a classic."

HARRIMAN, MARGARET CASE. *The Vicious Circle, The Story of the Algonquin Round Table*. New York: Rinehart & Co., Inc., 1951. Cites Stallings as "charter member" and as only war hero among the group.

HATCHER, HARLAN. *Creating the Modern American Novel*. New York: Russell & Russell, Inc., 1935. Claims that *What Price Glory?* "did more than any single novel on the same theme to define the point of view of the twenties."

HORNE, ALISTAIR. "What It's Like Over There." New York *Herald Tribune Books*, June 9, 1963, p. 5. Review of *The Doughboys*. Praises Stallings' personal touch, particularly his presentation of General Pershing.

KRUTCH, JOSEPH WOOD. *The American Drama Since 1918*. New York: Random House, 1939. The longest published treatment of *What Price Glory?*

"Laurence Stallings Dead at 73; 'What Price Glory?' Co-Author." New York *Times*, February 29, 1968, p. 37. Lengthy obituary reviews Stallings' career.

"Lest We Forget." *Saturday Review*, X (August 5, 1933), 25-27. Longest review of *The First World War* includes eight different commentaries.

MACLEISH, ARCHIBALD, and COWLEY, MALCOLM. "Lines for an Interment." *The New Republic*, LXXVI (September 20, 1933), 159-161. Debate on *The First World War* and its intended effect.

———. "The Dead of the Next War." *The New Republic*, LXXVI (October 4, 1931), 214-16. Continued debate about *The First World War*.

"Macon Playwright L. Stallings Dies." Atlanta *Journal*, February 29, 1968. Obituary.

MANTLE, BURNS, ed. *The Best Plays of 1924-25*. New York: Dodd, Mead and Company, 1925, 1955. Introduces and includes *What Price Glory?*

———. *The Best Plays of 1944-45*. New York: Dodd, Mead and Company, 1945. Includes summary of unpublished play, *The Streets Are Guarded*.

QUINN, ARTHUR HOBSON. *A History of the American Drama from the Civil War to the Present Day*. New York: Harper & Co., 1922. Criticizes profanity used in *What Price Glory?* Cites scene in "dugout cellar" as "masterly."

"Sandburg and Stallings." *Bookman*, LXIII (May, 1926), 261. Claims these two authors "sure to live in the literary history of this country. . . ."

SPILLER, ROBERT E., et. al. *Literary History of the United States*. New York: MacMillan & Co., 1949. Cites *What Price Glory?* as the most sensational play of 1924-25 season.

"Stallings Bored by Own Play Now." New York *Times*, October 30, 1936, p. 25. Portrait.

"Stallings on Way to Cover the War." New York *Times*, August 8, 1935, p. 7. Portrait; Ethiopian plans.

"Strange Screen Confidences." *Literary Digest*, XCII (March 5, 1927), 24. Reviews movie version of *What Price Glory?* Notes that language has been "cleaned up."

VIDOR, KING. *A Tree Is a Tree*. New York: Harcourt Brace, 1952. Devotes chapter to "The Big Parade"; credits Stallings with making him a successful director.

"WAR: Capt. Stallings Heads Fox-NANA Ethiopian Expedition." *Newsweek* (August 17, 1935), 31. Portrait; includes description of small caravan going to Ethiopia.

WATSON, MARK L. "They Were There, Lafayette." *Saturday Review*, XLVI (July 6, 1963), 28. Reviews *The Doughboys* as a "tale so moving that one can hardly lay it aside until it is finished."

Index